RETURN TO THE BIG RED ZONE

I0141424

Inside the Huskers' Winning 2016 Season

Steve Banner

Banner Business Services

Laguna Woods, CA

BOOKS BY STEVE BANNER

It's Only A Bike Race: How Hard Can It Be?

That Guy's Wearing Red, Too!

Steve Banner/Banner Business Services
805 Ronda Mendoza, Unit B
Laguna Woods, CA 92637
www.nebraskacollegefootball.com

Cover design by Holly Sosa

Book Layout © 2014 BookDesignTemplates.com

Return to the Big Red Zone / Steve Banner -- 1st ed.
ISBN 978-0-9864341-2-9

For dear Christi,
who opened the door to her heart and her culture.

"Not the victory but the action; Not the goal but the game; In the deed the glory."
HARTLEY BURR ALEXANDER
(Words from the former UNL professor of philosophy, inscribed on the southwest side of Memorial Stadium)

CONTENTS

THE HUSKERS ARE UNDEFEATED IN 2016!

Who knows what to expect for the coming season as I write these words in early September 2016? At this same time in 2015, my wife and I traveled to Omaha in preparation for the first game of the new season under a new Head Coach. Even

though we are at the end of the summer one year later, and about to transition to Fall, it feels more like Spring as we look forward to seeing the emergence of the shoots that have sprung forth from the seeds that were planted in the Nebraska football program some months ago.

The head farmer who took over control of the growing enterprise a year ago can now be said to be substantially in control. The effects of his efforts to train and guide the crop will become even more evident this year. Last year he did his best to work with the fields as he found them, but now they unmistakably bear his mark. Given the four-year cycle of this particular product, it would be unfair to say that the quality of all of the kernels in the harvest that springs from the fields this year can be credited to the skilled husbandry of Farmer Riley and his team, but more than a million statewide emotional and financial investors in the Big Red enterprise are hoping to reap a strong crop this year with the promise of even more outstanding harvests to come in each following year.

The off-season has indeed been difficult with the tragic loss of punter Sam Foltz. It was a joy to watch him on the field because unlike so many other punters, he could safely be relied upon to get his kick away not only safely but also with substantial distance.

As a former Australian Rules Football player, I can testify that these are essential skills that players start to develop at a young age and it takes years of practice to reach a consistent level of performance. When I first started to watch American Football in the 1990s I found it quite frustrating to watch the punters step mechanically forward like slow-motion robots after catching the snapped ball, seemingly unable to hurry their pace or adapt to the rush of defenders suddenly crowding in on them from all sides to block the kick.

Even at the NFL level, very few punters seemed to have mastered the skills required for their position. But Sam Foltz was an entirely different proposition as he received the snap and nimbly stepped forward while aiming and completing his kick, always finishing his follow-through safely long before any contact with a defender. His untimely demise is a loss not only to the Huskers but also to the NFL where he would have surely found a place.

Looking forward to the season ahead, I think I speak for all Husker fans when I say I hope it is not as "interesting" as last year when a number of games were lost in the final seconds. The ups and downs of the year provided me as a writer with ample opportunity to observe the character of Nebraska fans as they dealt with the unaccustomed adversity of an ongoing losing record throughout the year. I am pleased to say that the fans responded with a level of grace and maturity that would have been difficult to find in many other places, Dallas comes to mind as an example of a place where I found gracious losers to be few and far between. But this year I hope to be able to observe the other side of the equation: Nebraska fans as gracious winners.

May it be so.

CHAPTER ONE

CORNHUSKER BROTHERHOOD

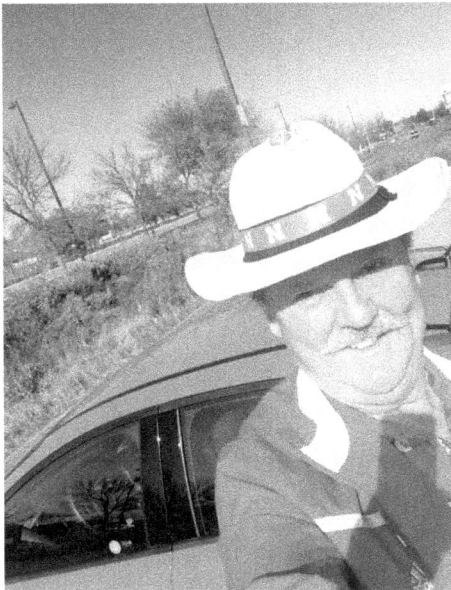

I've become convinced that there is no need for any such thing as a secret handshake in Nebraska. No matter where they are in the world, Nebraska fans can, at a distance, recognize one another as fellow members of the Cornhusker brotherhood by the color of their shirt, or at closer quarters, by the distinctive red letter "N" that has been placed surreptitiously on their clothing or even on their luggage. I know of that of which

I speak, because a few months before the season began I was flagged down by two visiting Americans who had spotted me across a crowded marketplace at a French Festival in downtown Sydney; and then once again at the busy Los Angeles International Airport while on my way to catch a flight for the opening game by Arthur, a Fremont native who now lives in the winterless suburbs of the City of Angels.

In all cases such as this, a lively conversation about the Huskers suddenly erupts out of nowhere like a flash flood down what only moments earlier had been a dry creek bed of silence. All parties concerned are immediately swept away at a frenetic pace as the discussion proceeds headlong from last week's game to the coming game and then eventually slows down to a more leisurely flow as introductions are made and hometowns are identified. In such encounters, the normal sequence of social protocol is turned on its head as the participants have recognized one another's *bona fides* to take part in a Nebraska conversation long before they are in close enough proximity to begin to speak. Thus, in contrast to the normal sequence of events in a conversation between parties who have just met for the first time, an animated discussion thus takes place at the outset, followed later by the usual niceties of introductions and small talk.

In situations such as these, I must confess that I am sometimes tempted to throw a spanner into the works by keeping a straight face, denying any connection to Nebraska and explaining to anyone who approaches me that what may at first appear to be a series of "N"s on my hatband is actually a series of "Z"s placed sideways in recognition of my alma mater Zane State College. It would be interesting to see the reaction from the person who approached me but I wouldn't have the heart to make up such a story because the enthusiasm with which I have been greeted in such settings is simply infectious and it would be rather churlish of me to deliberately prevent the floodgates of Husker-speak from opening with their usual rush.

And then there's the matter of one's sense of humor. My father-in-law Tom enjoyed a good laugh as much as anyone, but he was deadly serious when it came to his beloved Huskers. At one of the first games I attended, I recall asking him why there was a big red letter "Z" in the middle of the field. He didn't realize I was joking and curtly informed me that I was a letter "N" for Nebraska. I can only wonder what he must have thought about this dopey Aussie who could barely speak understandable English and wasn't even smart enough to read the alphabet properly. Thankfully, he kept such thoughts to himself as far as I know.

I soon learned Tom didn't have much of a sense of humor about his hometown of Omaha, either. One day on a family outing we were driving down one of the interstate highways that bisect the city when I remarked out loud that the city fathers were missing out on a fabulous revenue-raising opportunity.

"Instead of calling that road F Street" I began, "why don't they sell the naming rights to a sponsor? For example, F Street could now become McDonald's Boulevard".

Tom paused for a moment and then, with the kind of calm patience one normally reserves for small children and intellectually-challenged foreigners, gently explained that my idea would not work.

"Why not?" I asked in mock surprise.

"Because then nobody would be able to find F Street ", he replied.

I had no answer to that, but I knew how Vincent van Gogh must have felt as a great artist who was unappreciated during his own lifetime. My imaginative word pictures were going unsold just as his paintings had done, but at least I could content myself that my ears were so far intact.

Speaking of selling one's work, thanks to the generosity of Scott at Husker Hounds in Omaha I was able to spend a few hours in his store on the afternoon of the day before the 2016 opening game against the Fresno State Bulldogs signing copies of the book I had written about the 2015 season. Apart from this being a good location to offer copies of my book for sale, it was also an excellent location to observe and interact with Nebraska fans from near and far. While I watched, a steady stream of shoppers filed in, browsed around the shelves, crannies and corners of the cornucopia of Big Red memorabilia before finally making their way to the end of cash register line,

arms filled with all manner of crimson-colored articles intended for themselves and their families.

My wife, who had traveled with me, also enjoyed the spectacle and the conversations we were able to have with many of the shoppers, some of whom had driven from their homes in Colorado, Kansas and Oklahoma. We particularly enjoyed one charming older lady who was visiting from rural Iowa, where she lived. I had no reason to doubt her when she informed us that she had been raised in North Dakota, because when she spoke she sounded to me as if she were Lawrence Welk's slightly younger sister. She must have been in her early 80s, and apart from sharing Welk's German accent she also emanated the same sunny and smiling outlook that the famous bandleader had displayed throughout his many years of television productions.

It seemed that although she had traveled southwards from her original roots, she had not ventured far in a westerly direction because in her happy and optimistic way she breezily informed me that the entire state of Nebraska is "all tumbleweeds once you get past Lincoln". In her straightforward way, she apologized that she was not interested to buy my book because she was more of a fan of murder mysteries. She asked me whether I had plans for my next book to be of this genre, and I had to admit that I would find it hard to frame an account of the 2016 Huskers season in such a manner unless the lifeless body of Li'l Red was found hanging from the goalpost near the student section after the Homecoming Game. Nevertheless, before she left the store she encouraged me to "hang in there" with my writing. Perhaps I could learn a lesson from her and change the title of my earlier book to a more market-friendly "That Guy's Bleeding Red, Too"?

While we were still pondering how to weave a murder plot into the otherwise non-life-threatening world of college football, the familiar face of a man who really knows how to "hang in there" appeared at our elbow. Bob, our ticket man who always seemed to have a seat for me last season, had left his

post in Lincoln to drive over to see us in Omaha. He normally works his corner in Lincoln from 3pm to 7pm on the Friday before a game, buying tickets from fans who have spares available. But his tenacity really shines on a game day when he mans his outdoor "office" on 9th Street from 7am onwards buying and selling tickets and staying until as late as 7pm for evening games.

As we caught up on the news since the last time we had met, Bob talked about the Indy 500 and various college basketball and NASCAR events where he had plied his trade during the previous 9 months. In particular, he noted that he had been left with a handful of tickets to a recent premier NASCAR race that he had been unable to sell. To his experienced eye, this was clear evidence that the sport was in a serious and irreversible state of decline. "NASCAR is over", was his pronouncement. It was hard to dispute the validity of his conclusion when he showed me some of the high-face-value tickets that he was now using for bookmarks.

After the book signing was over we followed Bob's footsteps and drove to Lincoln in preparation for the next day's game. My father-in-law Tom had always talked about eating prairie oysters, and I hoped that we might find a place in the state's capital where I might for the first time try this Nebraska delicacy for myself.

As luck would have it, as we drew closer to our hotel we saw that a nearby steak house was displaying a sign offering as an appetizer the very dish that my wife's father would order at every available opportunity.

As has been the case for me ever since I first met my wife, my mind was completely open to a new Nebraska experience, but in this case I did not quite know what to expect as the waitress approached with the dish containing what I anticipated to be a very tasty treat. The objects themselves had been thinly sliced, battered, breaded and then deep fried. The resulting oval-shaped items were served with french fries, and the whole plate probably contained enough fat to clog the arteries of an entire family of elephants. There was a detectable and not disagreeable flavor in each "oyster" beneath the layers of grease, but as I ate I couldn't help but wonder how the French might prepare this particular dish.

It reminded me of the way my mother used to prepare lamb liver when I was young: it was edible but had the texture of rubber and eating it was never enjoyable. It wasn't until some

20 years later when I had the experience of eating liver in a French restaurant in Montreal that I learned that it could actually be quite delicious. I'm sure the same principle might apply to the aforementioned "oysters".

During the course of the evening we had the opportunity to chat with our waitress, a nice young lady who was about to start her senior year of college at the University of Nebraska with a Hospitality major. Naturally, the conversation turned to football and she told us that her schedule for the next day would be quite challenging as she had been invited to a friend's wedding at 4pm. She had apparently already warned her friend that she would have to leave the event early because the football game was scheduled to begin at 7pm.

"I'm not going to miss Opening Day in my senior year!" she asserted to us, leaving no room for any possible questions to the contrary.

Brittany told us she was planning to visit France and Italy for her winter break and was taken by complete surprise when we commented that she shared her name with a large part of the north-west region of France. We were glad that her major was not Geography, otherwise it might have been wise to ask for a refund of a significant portion of her tuition fees.

The Saturday morning newspapers were filled to the brim with anticipation for the first game of the season, rewarding the addictive cravings of Big Red fans everywhere who had been waiting since April's scrimmage game for another dose of football to feed their unshakeable habit. Two players in particular were featured in the coverage, both of whom were about to commence their senior season.

Josh Banderas, who is the son of former Husker tight end Tom Banderas, was expected to have a big year to cap a successful career that started in 2013 with him playing in every game as a true freshman.

Sam Hahn, a 6'7" 300-pound offensive lineman originally from DeWitt, had a rather different background. As a youngster growing up on the family farm he had always dreamed of playing football for Nebraska. However, he was overlooked by Big Red recruiters and began his collegiate football career at North Dakota State, which had offered him a partial scholarship and where he became part of the school's national championship team in 2012. But although his 6 feet 7 inch, 300-pound body might have been physically located in Fargo throughout that season, his heart remained deeply planted in Nebraska, and so in 2013 he returned to his roots and joined the Huskers' walk-on program. Even though he knew he would see far less playing time in a red uniform compared with the green of ND State, Hahn was determined to play out his college career with the Huskers regardless of how few and far between his on-field appearances might be. After three years at Nebraska, Hahn was scheduled to start his first game the next day. In many ways this would be a dream come true for the young man, yet he expressed himself very humbly when interviewed by the press, making it clear that he would make the most of this game in the knowledge that it may be the only start of his Nebraska career before he graduates in December and returns to the family farm.

The roster for the opening game was also affected by the absence of Nate Gerry and Brandon Reilly, two senior players who, according to Head Coach Riley, were suspended for the game as a result of their violation of unspecified team rules. While Reilly's absence could be covered by his fellow members of the receiving corps, Gerry's place as a key member of the defense was not so easy to fill.

With all of these personnel-related storylines in our minds, my wife and I set off for our usual rendezvous destination with Bob the Ticket Man and were pleasantly surprised to see that his business operations were now the beneficiary of a new and

relatively high-tech accessory in the form of a rather tersely-worded sign. Judging by the steady flow of people who stopped to talk with him on this intermittently rainy day, it would seem that Bob's sign was an outright success. It appeared to me that we were witnessing the validation of a phrase my father frequently used during my youth: "It pays to advertise if you've got the goods", although as I recall he used this phrase most often in response to the occasional appearance on the television of a scantily-clad swimsuit model.

Be that as it may, Bob seemed to be doing a brisk trade as we retired to the Red Onion Bistro for lunch. As was now our pre-game tradition, we toasted the memory of my wife's father with a red beer. Just to seal the deal, my wife ordered a Reuben sandwich, knowing as we now did that this famous creation had originated in Omaha and not New York as we had previously believed.

But New York was never far from the headlines in the news in the weeks leading up to football's Opening Day. The field for the ongoing Presidential Election race had narrowed considerably, and the two major party candidates both had strong ties to the Big Apple. As we walked towards the stadium before the game we passed the corner where midway through last season a small but enthusiastic group who called themselves "Nebraskans for Bernie" were holding up signs and handing out lapel stickers. My hope at that time had been that Bernie might get into office simply so that he could make his first order of business the issuance of an Executive Order that decreed all 2015 Nebraska football games be declared to have ended at the 14-minute mark of the fourth quarter. This would have resulted in an enormous improvement over the Big Red's dismal 5-7 regular season record that resulted from playing the final quarter all the way to 15 minutes.

Despite Bernie having dropped out of the race, I was heartened by the sight among the crowd of some newly-minted red shirts which had adapted the campaign slogan of one of the New York-based candidates. By the time we arrived at the stadium I had noticed only 5 or so Fresno State fans among the sea of red shirts, but sure enough once inside the stadium I could see that the fans of the visiting team - several hundred in number - had been safely shepherded into the south-west corner of the arena where they could make as much noise as they wanted. This was despite the daunting challenge of trying to out-yell the noisy and enthusiastic student section located nearby in the stadium's south-east corner.

It reminded me of Opening Day one year earlier when the visiting fans from BYU - who had arrived in much larger numbers than the Fresno State faithful - were divided in half and placed as far from one another as possible at the south-west and north-east corners of the arena. This, of course, was a wise and proactive move on behalf of the Memorial Stadium management to separate the visitors to prevent them from forming a single large Mormon group. Without this prudent precaution, they might have had enough people to form a choir which then started singing hymns during breaks in the game instead of songs like the Four Seasons' "Hey, Hey Baby!" that the rest of us attempted in our own off-key styles.

Unfortunately for them, the Fresno State fans did not have much to cheer about. In a lopsided affair, the home team built a 14-0 lead by early in the second quarter and eventually ran out victors with a final score of 43-10. The visitors had rallied to score 10 points before the halftime break, but were shut out with 29 unanswered points in the second half. The Huskers outrushed the Bulldogs 292-31 on the day, led by Devine Ozigbo with 17 carries for 103 yards and 2 touchdowns.

When interviewed after the game, Ozigbo commented that he although he thought the Huskers' play in the first half had been "a little sloppy", he felt the team just needs to "click" mentally because it has the skill and talent that are required to be successful.

The Huskers' game plan for the Bulldogs had been built heavily around the run, with a total of 51 rushing attempts for the day versus only 13 passing attempts. Nevertheless, quarterback Tommy Armstrong played a good game that continued on from his solid all-around performance in last year's Foster Farms Bowl. Although he only completed 6 of 10 passes against the Bulldogs, one of those passes was for a touchdown and he also ran for two touchdowns.

Although it was a convincing win for the Huskers, for various reasons not everyone was in a mood for celebration.

"I have a lot of real mixed emotions about the game." These were among the first words spoken by Head Coach Mike Riley at the post-game press conference. Although in this case Riley was referring to the uneven performance of his team on the field and their sometimes "sloppy" play, it had indeed been an emotional day for his players, coaches and the 90,013 spectators who had come to watch the opening game of the 2016 season.

On everyone's mind was the loss of Sam Foltz. While the team playbooks and coaching manuals are filled with detailed descriptions of how to respond to the myriad of different situations that may arise during a football game, there is surely no section of any of these manuals that deal with how to handle the loss of a key player during the off-season. Instead, Foltz's family, friends and teammates would have to improvise their own course of action to honor his memory. And with a little help from "upstairs" – and I don't mean the coaches' box in the West Stadium – they combined to create a very fitting and moving tribute to the memory of number 27.

Prior to the game, Drew Brown and Spencer Lindsay had carried Foltz's number 27 jersey out on to the field and raised it before the student section of the crowd, who cheered loudly. They then returned it to the sideline and draped it over the bench where it remained for the duration of the game. A little while later as Foltz's parents and family members watched from the sidelines, Sam's two little nephews Lane and Max walked through the tunnel with the players (who lifted them up to touch the horseshoe) and then led the team as they ran out on to the field together.

However, there was more to come on the fourth play of the game. Nebraska had the ball first but its opening drive stalled after 3 plays, and so the punt unit ran out on to the field. But in a surreal scene that few will ever forget, only 10 players lined up. Everyone was set in their assigned location except for the punter. The Huskers had created a "missing man" formation in the same way that Air Force pilots pay tribute to their fallen comrades by flying in a formation with a space left empty for their lost brother-in-arms. As the play clock ran down with the motionless players fixed in their positions, the enormous crowd rose to its feet and cheered for the memory of the missing man Sam Foltz. Tears flowed freely on the field, on the sidelines and in the stands.

When the clock finally ticked to zero, the officials threw a penalty flag for a delay-of-game. But in a classy move that will be appreciated by football fans everywhere, Fresno State declined the penalty. When talking about this moment after the game, the Bulldogs' Head Coach Tim DeRuyter choked back tears as he empathized with Nebraska and the way that he would feel if he lost his 23-year-old son, who is serving in the Air Force. Indeed the entire Fresno State team had worn "SF" decals on their helmets throughout the game to honor the memory of their fellow collegiate athlete.

Unbeknownst to many of the players on the field and certainly to my wife and me who were seated in the north-east corner of the stadium, there was a final word to be added to the Sam Foltz tribute. It had been raining prior to the game almost up until the kick-off, but finally the storm clouds moved away as the game got underway. Apparently, the missing man punt play had been sent "upstairs" for further review but, signaled by a rainbow that appeared to the north-west right after that play, the call on the field was upheld – or one might say it had received a blessing from above.

RIP Sam.

CHAPTER TWO

MOTHERHOOD AND APPLE PIE

"And then they charged us extra just to sit together. Can you believe it?" This was the lament by the couple I had just met in the Los Angeles airport as we walked together to catch our flight to Omaha on the Thursday night before the Wyoming game. As so often happens – and I never get tired of the warm feeling it brings me – the Nebraska-born pair had noted the hat-band which immediately identified me as a Husker fan and therefore a new friend with whom they could share what was on their mind. They had only decided a week earlier to attend their friend's wedding in Omaha, but they soon found that their flights were much more expensive than they had anticipated. By now they had committed to go to the wedding and thus they had no choice but to pay the asking price. I didn't have the heart to tell them that when I had checked online earlier in the day I had found that there were a lot of empty seats on the flight. Looking back on the situation, I just hope they enjoyed the

wedding and did not let the mysterious and unpredictable workings of the airline reservation system spoil their fun.

Meeting Nebraska fans at the airport reminded me of a day
during the previous season when I met three young adults who
were on their way from Dallas to watch their brother Devine
Ozigbo play I-back for the Huskers. The enthusiasm of his
brother and two sisters was infectious as they happily chattered
about Devine and his prospects for the coming game. As it
turned out, Devine's game time that day was limited to only a
handful of snaps and I felt sorry for his siblings who had traveled so far to see so little.

But what a difference a year makes, because in the first
game of the 2016 season Devine not only played most of the
game but was the team's leading rusher with 103 yards and two
touchdowns. I was happy for him and asked him at the press
conference after the game whether any members of his family
had been present at the stadium. To his credit, he responded
freely to what must have seemed like an odd question and said
that although none of them were there for the Fresno State
game, his brother and one of his sisters would be at the Oregon
game. I had not seen Devine at any of the 2015 press conferences, and so as far as I know this was his first such appearance.
He spoke articulately as he replied to questions from the press
corps, and seemed to be very poised with no sign of nervousness as he faced the dozen or so cameras aimed at him.

In contrast, last season I had seen a number of players who
were quite understandably uncomfortable to be behind a podium in front of the cameras and couldn't wait to escape the
spotlight. I can only imagine the pressure they feel as they are
asked to explain their actions, knowing that their words will be
reported to 1.8 million Nebraskans that night via television and

to countless more fans the next day via newspapers and the internet.

Thanks to the magic of modern technology, the words spoken at these press events are meticulously recorded. This, of course, is a great convenience for reporters as using a recording device allows them to concentrate more fully on the speaker rather than trying to keep up with the hopeless task of scribbling down notes as the subject of their questioning responds. I only wish I had been present at a press event that took place prior to

the first game when Coach Riley was reported to have uttered the following verbatim line that will live long in my memory: "We don't not redshirt players and then not play them."

Regardless of the context in which he made that statement, Riley had achieved the remarkable grammatical feat of crafting a triple-negative sentence in the space of a mere ten words. Both my school-teacher mother and newspaper editor grandfather would have been horrified to hear such a pronouncement, but personally speaking, I was delighted to have read it – albeit for a different reason.

Riley might have expressed his thought more correctly, if perhaps slightly less succinctly, as "It's not our policy to decline to give redshirts to players and then keep those players out of the game." But the fact that he spoke in the way that he did makes me glad to think that he feels at ease to share his unfiltered thoughts with the fans just as he would with friends. (Just like new friends he might meet at the airport who share the common Big Red bond.)

I drove to Beatrice the day before the Wyoming game with the aim of meeting up again with some of the friendly folks I had met there a year earlier. My first stop however was to meet Annie, a reporter from the *Beatrice Daily Sun* newspaper, for an interview. While we had a very pleasant chat over coffee at the Sunrise Bakery in the main street, I was particularly intrigued by a local delicacy that I had never encountered nor

could have ever imagined. Prominently displayed in the showcase was a special batch of doughnuts frosted with maple icing and covered with chopped bacon pieces. I can only imagine that this unlikely-sounding combination had originally been conceived by the wife of a baker who was heavily pregnant with twin potential Husker recruits and suffering from a craving for something sweet and yet savory at the same time. It reminded me of when my wife was pregnant with our son Tim, when her daily lunchtime craving was for a sandwich made with curried egg salad with sliced beets.

While a year earlier I had enjoyed a long conversation with Bob Sexton and his high school football coaching staff, Annie informed me that he was no longer doing the difficult dual task of coaching the football team and serving as vice-principal. A new head coach had taken over at the Beatrice Orangemen and I had the pleasure of watching his charges playing on TV later that evening at the American Legion post where I had gone in the hope of renewing acquaintances with some of the members I had met the year before.

As it turned out, I did indeed meet two club regulars with whom I had enjoyed conversations the year before. I was pleased to be able to give them both a copy of the book that had only been a gleam in my eye at our previous meeting. Or perhaps in their perception (and the perception of any rational person), all that talk about a book was more like a wild braggadocious idea from a crazy foreigner than anything else!

The tailgating crowd near the Holiday Inn was in fine form when I arrived in downtown Lincoln the next morning,. The ever-generous Mike and Jen were set up in their usual corner with a large TV screen in the back of the truck and an expansive array of culinary temptations. Continuing a long-standing tradition seen across the state, three generations of the family were present, with daughter Avery and Mike's father Brian all planning to go to the game. It was Mike's mother's turn to babysit Avery's sister, similar to how my wife's grandmother used to babysit my wife and her sister back in the 1960s while the parents went to the game.

Not long before the game, Mike asked me if I would like some apple pie. When I gladly accepted, he handed me a mason jar that contained what looked like a urine specimen. My first thought was of Jen, whom I had noticed had been drinking water that morning instead of partaking in the various range of cocktails on offer. This had made me wonder if she and Mike may have been trying to add a third little Husker fan to the brood, but I had no idea that I was to be exposed to the detailed physiological aspects of the family project. Mike must have seen the look on my face because he reclaimed the jar from me, removed the lid, and after inhaling deeply from the jar took a mouthful of the straw-colored contents.

"Here," he said as he gave the open jar back to me, "have a smell!" I meekly complied, too dumbfounded to think straight, and was greeted by the rich, earthy aroma of apple pie. I had never heard of a liquor called Apple Pie, but here it was under my very nose. As I took a sip of the warming liquid, one of the bystanders comfortingly assured me that it would cure coughs, colds and several diseases that I didn't even know I had.

Although he steered clear, or perhaps because he steered clear, of the apple pie and other concoctions that were being circulated, Bob the Ticket Man was in good form and hoping for a big win by the home team to help boost the level of interest in the following week's home game against Oregon.

Life from a Different Angle

It's amazing how different things look when you approach them from a new angle. Sometimes the simple rephrasing of a sentence makes an enormous difference to the reception of its intended audience: for example "I like to dine on steak and children" versus "I like children and dining on steak". But for the matchup against the Wyoming Cowboys, I had the opportunity to view the game from an entirely new perspective, both literally and figuratively speaking. An hour after the game my ears were still ringing and my knees were still aching, but the experience was worth the effort.

It all began by chance an hour or so before the game when a man came up to Bob the Ticket Man a few moments after I did and interrupted our conversation about the coming election by offering a single seat for sale, It turned out that Bob's only remaining tickets were in pairs, and so he suggested I buy the single ticket directly from the seller. I gladly did so, after Bob had negotiated a price, but I didn't realize until I had almost arrived at the Stadium that this seat was located in the midst of the Student Section, a.k.a. "The Boneyard", in the south-east corner near the band.

The first thing I realized as I was making my way to my seat was that it would be easy to get to my assigned spot because everyone was standing - but they were not simply standing, they were standing on the seats which made it much easier for me to walk between them to get to my spot. The hard part was when I tried to step up into my assigned place and was encountered by an irritated young lady who was thinking that I must be having a senior moment and had accidentally wandered off into the wrong part of the stadium.

"This is the student section" she informed me in an impatient tone devoid of any sense of pity for the poor old geezer who had so obviously lost his way.

"Yes, I know" I feebly replied as I stepped up on to what now seemed to be a very narrow plank that serves as seating space for everyone in the stadium with the apparent exception of this particular demographic group.

"I bought my ticket on the street", I ventured by way of an attempt at an explanation of how I had come to find myself surrounded by a lively horde of fervent youngsters embracing the "college football experience" on a beautiful day in what felt like late summer. I might as well have saved my breath.

With an annoyed sigh she moved further to her left to be more distant from me and closer to her friends, and then turned back to her phone. I tried to look out the corner of my eye to see if she was sending a text to the closest Senior Care Center to ask them to do a quick headcount to make sure all of their patients were accounted for. But she soon forgot about me when a wasp inconveniently flew into our immediate vicinity and created scenes of ducking and weaving pandemonium that would have made the boxer Bud Crawford proud.

I was soon to learn that the students were accustomed to following a number of different traditions and rituals during their game-watching experience. The first of these that I was to wit-

ness was the kick-off routine which unfolded after the Huskers scored their first touchdown, As the players lined up on the field for the ensuing kick-off, the hundreds of students around me took off their right shoe, lifted it high above their head, and jabbed it rhythmically in the air in time with their singing until the moment the ball was kicked.

Perhaps it was the fact that I was feeling like a complete fish out of water in this environment that made me look around for any signs of departure from this uniformly-observed practice, but I did spot one dissenter in the crowd several rows ahead of me. This particular misfit wore boots instead of shoes, and then as if to further underline his non-conformist stance he held up his left boot instead of his right. We can only hope that this kind of wayward thinking was duly noted by the young lady next to me, soon to result in a stern lecture from her to be delivered to the radical troublemaker hiding in the midst of the student body.

But just as some traditions were observed with an almost religious zeal, others were notable by their absence. Just as I had encountered in other parts of the stadium and at last year's bowl game, I am sad to say that there was no singing of the fight song after each touchdown even though the Huskers created a total of seven such singing opportunities during the course of the afternoon. I would have tried to lead the way by singing the song loudly to try to encourage participation, but after my arrival experience I didn't dare to risk being hauled off in a large butterfly net as I sang forlornly to myself in the midst of stunned silence all around me.

But I was also distracted after that first touchdown as I waited for everyone to sit down. But no-one did. We continued to stand of the seats that wobbled a bit sometimes as people moved or danced in place to the PA music that seemed to elicit much more reaction in this part of the stadium than I had seen in other parts. I thought to myself "Even if we do want to stand throughout the game, why not stand on the concrete floor instead of the seats? The view would still be the same for everyone and the footing would be much more stable."

I quickly realized that if I had expressed the above thought aloud, I would have sounded like my father, and everyone else's father - which of course would have answered my own question as to why the crowd was not following what seemed like a more sensible course of action.

When the second quarter came to a close, the entire section of fans immediately sat down, almost in unison. We all retained the same view we had enjoyed only moments earlier but those of us with aging knees were suddenly much more comfortable. I wondered why we wouldn't now sit from this point on, but then that's what our fathers would have advised us to do. After a well-executed Hawaiian-themed half-time performance by the band we all jumped back up on to our seats – some in more spry fashion than others.

Looking back I realize that I was lucky not to have found a vendor before the game from whom to rent a seat cushion and back for $5. I don't know what I would have done with said item (perhaps I could have stood on it and eased the pressure on my feet and knees, but then I would have felt guilty as if I were standing on someone's sofa).

My educational experience continued during the third quarter when I was privy to observe the inner workings of a sporting phenomenon that has long intrigued me: namely, "The Wave".

Where does it come from and who starts it? Those had always been my questions as I watched thousands of people rise and fall in unison around a stadium as if they were the fabric on a carpet that was being shaken out by a housekeeper with a short attention span. Up until today, the only thing I knew about The Wave was that if you start one at the Melbourne Cricket Ground in Australia you will be ejected and invited to never return. That kind of bureaucratic joy-killing reminds me of when I lived in Florida around the time that the Florida Panthers hockey team was launched. Early in the team's first season, several fans threw their hats out on to the ice right after one of the visiting players had scored his third goal of the game. In a remarkably quick response, security guards quickly found the rabble-rousers responsible and threw them out of the stadium. Apparently, the guards were completely unaware of hockey's long-standing hat-trick tradition.

But on this day in Lincoln, I was privileged to be right in the midst of the instigators of the wave that swept Memorial Stadium during the third quarter. The early ripples began in the student section, and after several false starts the wave took off in earnest around the stadium as we all forgot about the action on the field. After several brisk revolutions, the order was given to make the next wave slow - and as if the instructions had

been sent by mental telepathy, the next circumnavigation proceeded at a slow-motion snail's pace. By the time the wave returned to its student originators the word had gone out to switch to Warp speed, and 89,895 people responded accordingly as they quickly stood, waved their arms like quick-action characters in a silent movie and then sat down again. Even the yellow-clad Wyoming fans who had been herded into their own visitors' ghetto in the corner of the stadium took part.

During the game - especially the last quarter - the crowd had plenty of reasons to cheer their Huskers. There was a total of five interceptions by Nebraska, each of which drew what was to me an almost deafening roar. The reaction of the crowd was certainly not lost on the players, who often turned and gestured to the Student Section during the game to get them to cheer. Watching the game from among the students was quite invigorating and gave me a whole different perspective that I had not previously held since I did not attend the University of Nebraska. It also provided me with some insight into what my wife's experience might have been like as a student in the 1980s.

I wondered if she had been a right-shoer or a lefty? Either way, the answer would explain a lot of things about her.

The game itself began slowly with the Huskers leading 7-0 at the end of the first quarter, and 17-7 at the half. By the time the 3rd quarter ended the home team's lead was only 24-17 despite having intercepted the Cowboys quarterback twice during the quarter. The final quarter saw three more interceptions by the Blackshirts, resulting in a final score of 52-17. Bob's wish for a large margin of victory had been granted, but it had not been as dominant a performance as the final score might have suggested.

After the game, Head Coach Riley was in a much better mood than had been the case one week earlier when he had complained about "sloppy" play. Nevertheless, he voiced his disappointment at the single interception thrown by Huskers QB Armstrong.

Tommy Armstrong too seemed much happier than the previous week when he had spoken very softly with his head down and had the demeanor of someone who felt he had let his team down, rather than having thrown for one touchdown and run for two more. This week he was much more upbeat, having thrown for three touchdowns (to become Nebraska's all-time leader in that category) and running for one. In his typically humble fashion, he deflected from himself any hint of praise from the press and gave the credit to his blockers and receivers.

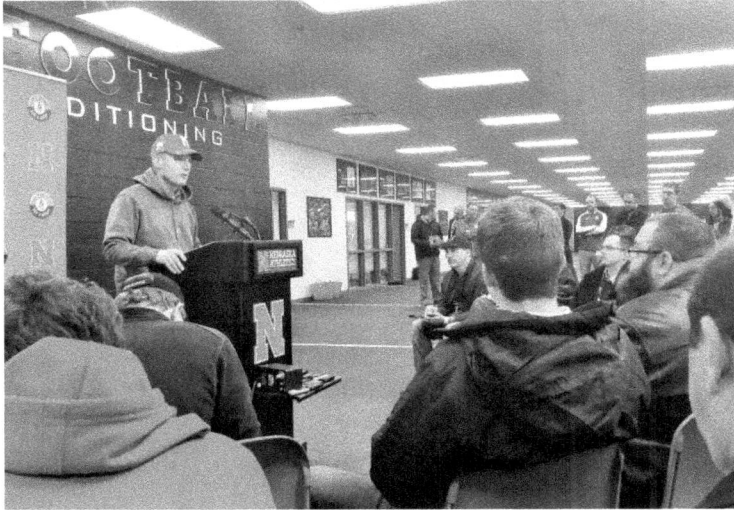

Watching the game from the Student Section was by far the most entertaining experience in the Husker crowd that I had ever had. It would be very interesting to compare it to the experience of watching the game from Larry the Cable Guy's private box, but I'm not sure if I would really want to share the same confined space if Larry removed his shoe before every kick-off!

From the Beatrice Daily Sun

"Husker book to include Beatrice chapter

Annie Bohling Daily Sun staff writer Sep 9, 2016

A new book about Nebraska and its affair with college football written by an Australian native will have a chapter devoted to Beatrice.

Sitting in Sunrise Bakery on Friday and dressed in a button-up, short-sleeved red shirt printed with Nebraska Cornhuskers football symbols, author Steve Banner explained the project.

The new book is a sequel to his prior work, titled, "That Guy's Wearing Red, Too!" The title is something Banner said in 2001 when first exposed to the "Husker Nation."

From that point on, Banner's fascination with Nebraskans' pride in their state and their football team grew, prompting him to write a book, which he described as an exploration of Nebraska and "its unique football tradition."

The sequel is an extension of that exploration.

Banner is continuing his journey by attending all Husker home football games this season from different sections of the stadium, watching away games in Husker fan bars in Los Angeles, San Francisco, Phoenix and Dallas, and interacting with neighboring Husker fans in those settings.

He's also visiting small towns to visit with Nebraskans about their memories and affection for the Cornhuskers. That's where Beatrice comes in.

Banner married an Omaha native, Christine, in 2003. Her mother is a Beatrice native. A chapter dedicated to Beatrice will include anecdotes from natives about their recollections of Nebraska life and favorite memories of Husker football he gathered in his visit to town.

One memory that stands out in Beatrice for Banner is a long talk with former Beatrice High School football coach Bob Sexton, who explained his philosophy of using football as a means to help develop character. Banner, a fan of that philosophy, noted that it's echoed by Nebraska head coach Mike Riley.

Other chapters will follow the same model with the setting in towns such as Scottsbluff, Osceola, Sidney, Norfolk and McCook.

"One thing I want to explore is people's recollections of Nebraska football game days as kids, and traditions on those days," Banner said.

For this book, he also hopes to interview two famous Husker fans -- Warren Buffett and Larry the Cable Guy, whose real name is Daniel Whitney.

Highlights of the season and answers from Husker football players and coaches at press releases attended by Banner will also be worked into the book.

"A message to take away from this book is that you Nebraskans have something very special here and you might not appreciate how quite special it is," Banner said. "The more I visit, the more I understand just how special it is."

Banner described himself as a keen sports fan who has attended iconic sports events across the world.

"But none are like this -- none are like going to a Husker game," he said. "The atmosphere of it, the feel of it. The balloons, the bands. People are so friendly and warm. You can see the good sportsmanship of the players. It's unique. The state and the football team are such huge parts of everyone's identity, it feels like to me."

Banner said Nebraskans must be generous, hard-working and considerate of their neighbors due to their ancestral roots as immigrants and homesteaders.

"The generosity of spirit and good-natured pride of Nebraska fans are what brought me here in the first place, and that's why I've come back again," Banner said in a press release. "I have met so many wonderful and genuine people in my travels across the State so far, and I can't wait to meet more of them as I travel further west to places like Scottsbluff and listen to their tales."

For more information about Banner's current and future books, visit his blog, NebraskaCollegeFootball.com."

CHAPTER THREE

DUCK SOUP IN LINCOLN

Duck Soup was exactly what Nebraska fans were hoping for when the University of Oregon football team came to town for the third game of the season. A couple of days before the game,

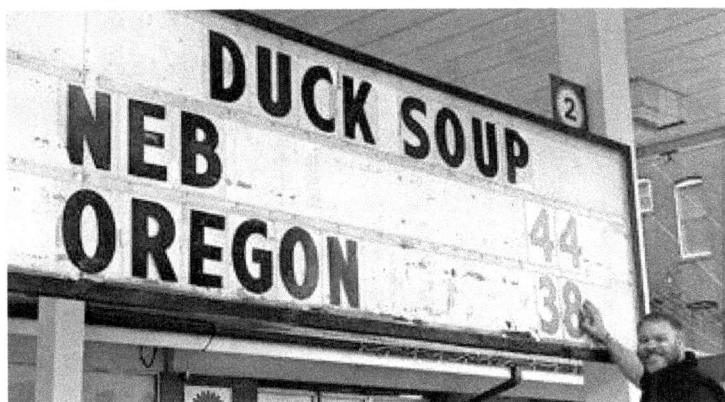

the score had already been forecast and posted on the board outside the popular gas station on 9th Street that fills to the brim with faithful tailgaters every game day. The fact that the Ducks had played for the national championship only two years earlier and were now ranked no. 22 in the national polls was of no concern to the Husker fans, as they recalled how their intrepid lads had beaten a much higher-ranked Michigan State team last year in Lincoln.

Although I am by nature an optimist, I must confess that I did not think the Huskers would be able to beat the Ducks without assistance and so I called on Lily the mini huskerhound for

help. She always wears a Nebraska scarf each game day but for this week my wife added an extra good luck item to her pre-game routine in the form of a squeaky duck toy that she worked on doggedly throughout the day.

This Oregon matchup looked by far to be the most important of the Huskers' home games for the season. A victory against this highly-regarded opponent would provide a much-needed boost of confidence to the players and coaches as they looked ahead to the tough opponents they would face on the road in Wisconsin, Ohio State and Iowa. Even a close loss to the Ducks would likely offer some consolation, given the strength of the Oregon program over the past few years. In other words, a fascinating contest was shaping up, and for serious Husker fans this looked like a game not to be missed.

Except I managed to miss it.

It wasn't easy, but somehow I managed to get my weeks mixed up and made my travel arrangements for Scottsbluff instead of Lincoln. I had wanted to make a trip to Scottsbluff before the cold weather set in, but by the time I discovered I had chosen the wrong dates in the calendar it was too late to correct my mistake. And so it was on a Thursday night that I found myself at Los Angeles International waiting for a flight to Denver instead of Omaha when I almost got the chance to meet a Ducks fan.

I had seen the mid-40ish man wearing an Oregon cap, walking through the concourse on his way to board the 6.40pm Omaha flight. I tried my best to make contact with him but there was no response. I called out to him again: "Hello! Oregon fan?" but he kept walking with his head down, oblivious to my overtures. I wanted to wish him a good trip to Omaha and an enjoyable time at the game but he kept walking without so much as a sideways glance.

It reminded me somewhat of one of those cartoons where Donald Duck would lose his temper over one thing or another and then stomp away muttering to himself under his breath.

Maybe this particular guy was thinking "*Sassafrass*! I fly all the way to Nebraska for a dumb football game and those pesky Cornhuskers beat us by a touchdown!"

Time would, of course, be the ultimate judge of my off-handed prediction, but it also reminded me of last season when I met an energetic retired couple just before the Michigan State game who had driven all the way from Michigan to watch their team take on the Huskers. After hearing about their drive through the various states I told them that I was sorry for them that their return trip would not be quite as pleasant after traveling all this way just to see their team lose. I was joking of course (and fairly convinced that it would be the Huskers who would lose). When I thought about the similarity between the two incidents I hoped that the pattern of a loss by the visiting team would be repeated on Saturday.

I had always wanted to visit Scottsbluff because it is where my wife's great-aunt Helen Heller used to live. She had been born to homesteader parents in Hooper, NE and grew up in that area before marrying and moving to the west of the state. This was to be my first trip to the western side of Nebraska, and I would enter the state from the south by car after flying into Denver.

By sheer good fortune, I must have chosen the best possible route because did not see any evidence of the endless plague of tumbleweeds that Lawrence Welk's sister had warned me about so sternly a couple of weeks earlier that carpet the countryside west of Lincoln. I hadn't seen any of the offending objects last year on my trips to Grand Island and Kearney, but I had simply figured that the I-80 had been safely cleared by a fleet of tumbleweed plows that are later converted into use each winter as snow plows.

Although I noted that hills and bluffs of the landscape as I drove north into Nebraska from Colorado were quite different in comparison to the areas I had seen in the east, I was interested to see something completely new to me. While I had been vaguely aware that sugar beets are a crop that is widely grown in this part of the state, I had never seen an actual sugar beet.

This gap in my education was quickly filled when I arrived in Scottsbluff because my hotel was near a sugar mill and the harvest season was well underway. Surrounding the mill were

enormous piles of brown-colored objects that looked like bocce balls, lying in wait for the front-end loaders that would scoop them up and carry them off for processing,.

But this discovery on my part also led me to wonder about something else. If Nebraskans from the eastern parts of the state are called Cornhuskers, does that mean those from the western parts are called Beetniks?

Regardless of the distance between my recent travels, I encountered the same universally friendly spirit in Scottsbluff as I had in Aurora, Hooper and other parts of Nebraska.

For example, not long after I arrived in Scottsbluff I stopped into a salon near the center of town for a haircut. When I mentioned to the hairdresser Brandi that I was planning to watch the game at the Union Bar (which I had found online) in nearby Gering, she was very happy to tell me what to expect when I arrived to watch the game.

She also shared her favorite menu item as well as that of her husband. In addition, she was kind enough to warn me in advance about the house specialty ironically known as the "Diet Burger". After hearing about the bar and its creative menu options, I was looking forward to the next day's game more than ever.

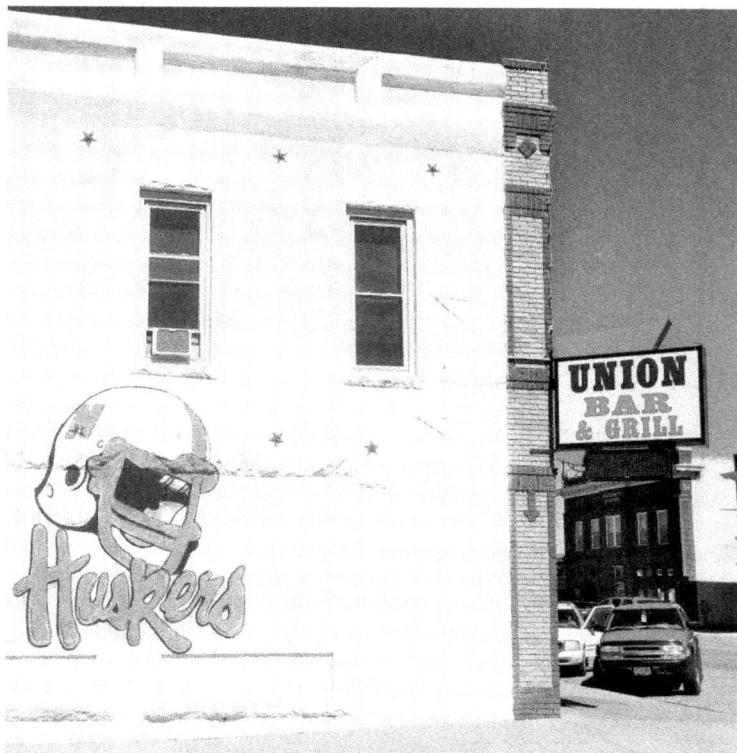

Waddle the Ducks Do?

That was the question that Nebraska fans were asking themselves before the game, just as they were wondering what the Huskers could possibly do to stop the explosive and unpredictable offense that Oregon had developed over the past few years. Visions of long Oregon runs down the field and missile-like passes danced through the heads of the Huskers faithful before the game. And it wasn't long before those nightmare scenarios became a reality.

By the time there were 2 minutes and 30 seconds left in the first half, the Ducks had already unleashed a myriad of their signature *blitzkrieg* plays and the score was 20-7 in their favor, thanks in part to a 50-yard touchdown run that made the Huskers' defense look like a stationary, termite-riddled, picket fence. The Ducks had easily succeeded in scoring a two-point conversion after their first touchdown, but their subsequent attempts fell short – otherwise, the score would have been 24-7. Nevertheless, they held a 13-point margin and looked like running away with the game.

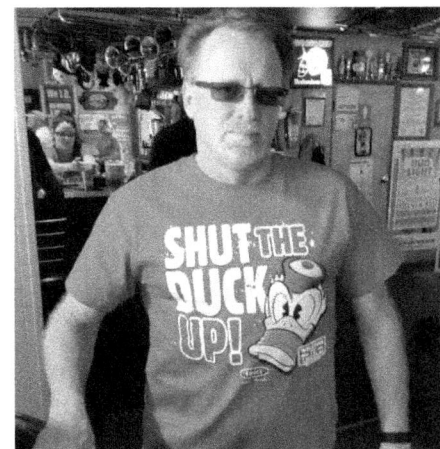

The crowd at the Union Bar in Gering was following the game intently, and even though I had found myself in the Scottsbluff area by accident after mixing up my dates, I was enjoying the gameday atmosphere that made me feel as if I were in Lincoln as I had originally intended. Upon walking in I had been warmly welcomed by the group of regular patrons who filled a room to one side of the main bar area and had been warming up with shots since 10am for the 1.30pm kickoff.

I had experienced a game day among Husker fans outside of Nebraska many times before, but this was to be the first time that I had experienced a game day 400 miles from Lincoln while still being in Nebraska. The owners of the Union Bar clearly took their responsibility seriously and made sure there were plenty of screens available to watch the game, while also offering a free chili and bratwurst buffet prior to the game. Even more fitting for the occasion, the owner Scott passed around sliced smoked duck leg cutlets during the game.

In the interests of full disclosure, I must admit that I did not properly fulfill my obligations as a gracious guest in this regard because I only had limited room to accommodate these very flavorsome duck treats. My logistical problem in this sense had stemmed from an earlier conversation with a regular customer named Eric, to whom I had mentioned that I wanted to take a photo of the almost legendary Diet Burger that Brandi the hairdresser had told me about. With his hospitable nature, Eric immediately insisted that he buy me a Diet Burger so that I could not only take a photograph of the house special but also have the opportunity to enjoy it with my taste buds.

Chef Jeremy was justifiably proud of his caveman culinary creation which contains a total of one pound of hamburger meat, copious amounts of bacon and uses two grilled cheese sandwiches on Texas toast in the place of hamburger buns, and is served with French fries for good measure. (And now dear reader, I'm sure you can understand why room in my stomach

for further snacks such as smoked duck meat was severely restricted – even though I only ate about 60% of Jeremy's
imposing Column of Cholesterol.)

Contrary to my better judgment, I felt hungry to tackle the
Diet Burger even though I knew only too well about the un-
healthy elements of excess that were lurking within the Tower
of Terror that Jeremy had set before me with such a triumphant

flourish. Each mouthful tasted salty, crunchy, juicy, greasy, and
above all delicious. In other words, I had encountered the very
epitome of guilty pleasure on a plate.

After fighting my losing battle with the Diet Burger, I recalled that Brandi had told me how she and her husband happened to be sitting in the bar one evening when two slim and "dainty" young ladies, as she described them, came in from out of town and wanted to order dinner. After looking over the menu they both decided on the Diet Burger because they wanted to eat something light. Brandi's immediate impulse was to warn the two visitors that the name of the dish they had ordered was by no means an accurate indication of its contents, but her husband persuaded her to remain quiet because he wanted to see the look on their faces when their plates of choice were delivered. The result must have been priceless!

Jeremy, who has cooked at the Union Bar for the past 6 years, also told me about another original creation of his that graces the menu: the pork-based "Boargasm Sandwich". I could imagine that many people would order such an exotically-named dish just to find out what was in it or to see if it lived up to the promise of its name. However, I had already been soundly defeated by Jeremy's flagship creation and had neither room nor desire left for further exploration in the culinary world according to Jeremy.

Meanwhile, the game had not gone so well for the Huskers, but regular bar patron Sal piped up from time to time to try to ease the tension with his comic-relief proposal "Let's switch to the NASCAR". (I guess he hadn't heard the news from Bob the Ticket Man that NASCAR is "over".) This was a recommendation that he made on several occasions during the dismal moments of the first half but he was momentarily silenced when Armstrong passed to Westerkamp 5 seconds before the half to score a touchdown and make the score a more respectable 20-14 at the long break.

During the half-time break, one of the regular patrons passed around the bacon-wrapped jalapeno poppers that he had made using peppers that he had grown at home. As much as my stomach was already groaning, I felt I had to find some room for these local treats and I was not disappointed for having made the effort.

After the half, it was a different game as Devine Ozigbo came into play and made a number of important rushes for his team. I was happy to recall his response to my question from a couple of weeks ago when he said that he would have several family members at the Oregon game. I'm sure that they were proud of their brother with his 21 carries for 95 yards, most of which took place in the second half of the game.

When Ozigbo ran for a touchdown halfway through the third quarter the score was 28-20 for the Huskers and the mood in the Union Bar was upbeat, to say the least. I was happy to sing along when the fight song was played after each touchdown, and even though no-one else joined in I did not feel self-conscious in the way that I had at the stadium in Lincoln and elsewhere. Perhaps it was the red jello shots that the bar owner's wife passed around after each touchdown that boosted my confidence!

With all the scoring that had taken place, it had become evident before the half that the result of the game would come down to the team that had the ball last. Oregon had scored two touchdowns to take a 32-28 lead with 10 minutes left in the game and would have been further ahead except for their four failed two-point conversion tries.

Armstrong had played a good game and had carried the ball for significant yardage but had also suffered a number of blows from hard tackles. It was unclear whether he could continue and at one point he had been replaced by Fyfe. But with the game on the line with 3 minutes left in the fourth quarter and the ball on the Huskers' 48-yard line, he stepped up and completed a crucial 14-yard pass to Westerkamp on 4th and 9 to keep the Huskers' final drive alive.

And then two plays later, Armstrong kept the ball on a designed run and scampered 34 yards into the end zone for what would be the game-winning touchdown. The final score was 35-32 in favor of the Huskers and the crowd at the Union Bar savored the victory with high fives and spirited cheers. Meanwhile, the Oregonians must have pondered what might have happened if they had contented themselves with a single point after each of their 5 touchdowns instead of pursuing the false promise of a two-point conversion. They must also have wondered about their 13 penalties for 126 yards that allowed the Huskers to maintain their momentum at critical points in the game. In comparison, the comparatively well-behaved Nebraskans had just 7 penalties for 55 yards.

It was an important win for the Huskers which not only brought their record to 3-0 but also put them in sight of a 9- or 10-win regular season, which must have felt very encouraging to the players and coaches after last year's losing season with only 5 wins during the entire regular season.

As much as I enjoyed being part of the enthusiastic crowd at the Union Bar, I wished that I could have been there to witness the post-game press conference in Lincoln during which I expect that a certain Head Coach may have been smiling. Even more entertaining would be the sight of flocks of Ducks fans "*sassafrassing*" to themselves under their breath as they left the stadium!

Diet Burger

Ingredients
1 pound hamburger meat
12 slices thick cut bacon
2 slices American cheese
2 slices Swiss cheese
4 slices thick cut white bread "Texas toast"

Method
Divide hamburger meat into three equal patties. Cook burger patties and bacon. Use bread and cheese to create two grilled cheese sandwiches in which each contains 1 slice of each type of cheese and 2 slices of bacon. Using one grilled cheese sandwich as the base, place 2 slices of bacon on top and then stack the 3 burger patties with 2 slices of bacon between each patty. Put 2 bacon slices on the 3rd patty and place the remaining grilled cheese sandwich on top. Skewer the completed stack with a steak knife and serve with French fries, onion rings and pickles.

Boargasm Sandwich

Ingredients
6 ounces smoked pork, shredded
1 thick slice of ham, drizzled with barbecue sauce
2 thick slices of bacon
2 large onion rings
Brioche bun

Method
Cut the bun in half and lightly toast both halves. Place 1 onion ring on lower bun base, followed by ham, sauce and cooked bacon. Top with the remaining onion ring and the upper half of the bun.

CHAPTER FOUR

I'VE SEEN THE PROMISED LAND

Such was my feeling as I drove south from Scottsbluff early on the Sunday morning after the Oregon game. I was heading south towards Colorado, and as I started to descend from the broad plateau on which Scottsbluff rests, a vast and verdant valley opened up ahead of me with a fertile plain that extended as far as the eye could see.

Where else could such a land of milk and honey be found except in Nebraska, and what better place than in the county that was so obviously named after me? The Almighty was clearly sending me a message that I should lead my wife and mini huskerhound to settle in this promised land.

I wonder if He would mind if we continued to spend our winters in California?

Thoughts of idyllic summer and spring seasons in rural Banner County, interrupted only by occasional forays into Gering for Diet Burgers and red beer served with grilled sliced sugar beet, danced through my head as I drove on towards my ultimate destination of Denver. But somewhere in the countryside west of Fort Morgan my reverie came screeching to a halt with a large dose of reality that hit me square in the eye. There to my right was a 40-foot reminder that there is another world outside the protected bubble of college football.

After getting back home and reviewing the videotape of the Oregon post-game conference, I could see that Coach Riley was indeed smiling after the Huskers extended their perfect record to 3-0 with their hard-fought win over the Ducks. No slow-motion replays were needed to confirm my assessment, nor views from different angles: he and his players were very pleased with their performance, as they had every right to be.

During the last season and this, I have seen that Riley's overall philosophy is reflected in his even-keeled and controlled reaction after each game. He was criticized last season by some fans – unfairly in my opinion – for his low-key reaction after several tough losses. According to these shortsighted individuals, he should have been more visibly upset.

And then following some winning games where these same fans expected him to be riding the same jubilant roller coaster that they were on, Riley would reflect on the parts of the game that did quite not go according to plan, and then turn the discussion to the next game.

It seems to me that the essence of Riley's response to the inevitable ups and downs of each season is quite sensibly based on his view of the entirety of his team's schedule. To overreact to a single day in which the team goes 1-0 or 0-1 makes no sense when it is the overall win-loss tally at the end of the season that counts for conference and bowl rankings.

On the other hand, I have seen cases where this unemotional approach can be taken to an extreme. For example, when my hometown Australian Rules Football team the Adelaide Crows made history by winning the national championship in the mid-90s, it was an event of great import for the entire state of South Australia. With about 1 million inhabitants, the state had the second-lowest population among the six states in the country and had been a perennial underdog in national sporting events for as long as anyone could remember. As a result, the reaction in the state capital of Adelaide to the Crows winning the national championship was exuberant, to say the least, with ticker tape parades and keys to the city awarded to the entire team.

The Crows repeated the feat the next year, and although the reaction in the streets of Adelaide was no less enthusiastic, the Head Coach took the wind out of the sails of the players immediately after the game when asked whether the Crows could possibly make it three-in-a-row the next season. To paraphrase his zen-like response, which he delivered live on national TV during the trophy presentation, he said: "Well this was a good win today, and I'm happy for the players. But in the overall scheme of life, it doesn't matter, and it won't matter whether or not we do it again next year." When I heard these words I thought it must have been incredibly demotivating for the players, and many of them must have questioned why they had worked so hard for a coach who didn't seem to care whether they won or lost. Not surprisingly, the Crows did not even make it to the playoffs that following year.

For reasons such as this, I was glad to see Coach Riley smiling and encouraging his players to enjoy their Oregon win for the next 24 hours before getting back to work to face Northwestern.

The lively crowd at the Union Bar in Scottsbluff was not shy to demonstrate their feelings after the Oregon game, and the next few days gave me the option to celebrate a potential Huskers win against Northwestern in a completely different manner. Business took me to Las Vegas for a few days after the Oregon game, and it occurred to me that I ought to make use of the opportunity to place a bet on the coming matchup. The

Huskers were listed as a 7-point favorite, and I would think that the sign outside the Philips 66 station in Lincoln that predicts the score each week probably had the Big Red winning by 10 points or more. If ever there was such a thing as a good bet in Las Vegas, it appeared to me that a wager on the Huskers would fit the bill. The only problem is that I got side-tracked when I bumped into a certain politician. We started to talk about what he would do as President, but when I asked him about his preferred Cabinet position he replied "Next to the dining room table".

By the time I had finished pondering the impenetrable wisdom of his answer, I never got around to placing my bet on the football. And heaven knows there is no way I would ever want to bet on the outcome of the election!

Trumping the Wildcats

"Make Nebraska Great Again" was the slogan printed on a line of t-shirts and hats on display at Husker Hounds in Omaha, and it also seemed to be the mantra of Tommy Armstrong and his troops as they extended their season's unbeaten record to 4 games by beating Northwestern 24-13 and making me regret that I had failed to act on my impulse of betting on the Big Red.

Playing away from home at Ryan Field in Evanston, Illinois, the Huskers must have almost felt like they were playing to an empty stadium with a mere 40,284 spectators in attendance in comparison to the 90,000 or so enthusiastic fans who had watched their first three games of the season.

Tommy Armstrong's performance was "yuge" as certain persons might say, with a personal best rushing performance of 132 yards in addition to his 246 passing yards. Had it not been for two bizarre plays in which a Huskers player lost control of the ball just as he was about to cross the goal line for a touchdown, the margin between the teams would have been even greater at the end of the day.

The lively crowd of Californians for Nebraska who had assembled at Danny K's Billiards and Sports Bar in Orange CA groaned in unison as Terrell Newby fumbled the ball while diving for the goal line early in the first quarter, only to groan again late in the 2nd quarter when Devine Ozigbo lost the ball as he tried to force his way through the Wildcats defenders at the goal line. Without these two mishaps, the score would have been 24-7 in favor of the Huskers at the half instead of 10-7.

Official University of Nebraska Alumni Chapter

But there was plenty of action during the half-time break to keep the Danny K's crowd entertained as a variety of Huskers goodies and memorabilia was raffled off to raise money for the club's scholarship fund.

Speaking as someone fortunate enough to have grown up in a warm climate, I couldn't help but feel for the handful of unsuspecting young Californians who are awarded funds each year to help them on their way to studying at the University Nebraska. Of course, everything is fine when they leave sunny California and land in Lincoln in late August, but by the time the Nebraska winter sets in it's too late for them to request tuition refunds and they have no choice but to bundle up and endure the frigid darkness that follows the football season. I must confess to contributing in a small way to this bait-and-switch racket when I bought some tickets in the raffle and donated a couple of my "That Guy's Wearing Red, Too!" books as prizes. I had my eye on the fabulous fuzzy dice prize, but alas my number did not come up and I was forced to drive home with an embarrassingly unadorned rearview mirror.

But for the 30ish couple Michael and Monica that I met just before the game began, their number had come up big earlier in the year. This lucky pair were the winners of the Californians for Nebraska off-season raffle in which the first prize was a trip for two to the opening game in Lincoln.

However, this unforeseen stroke of good luck caused an immediate concern for the couple as they had already made arrangements to go the Oregon game in week 3 of the season, and they did not fancy the thought of making two cross-country trips in the space of three weeks. But after further review, as the saying goes, the dilemma was resolved when the pair decided to simply drive up for the first game and stay with friends outside Lincoln for a few weeks until after the Oregon game.

Thus, in one foul swoop, these two dedicated Nebraska fans had solved their problem to the satisfaction of all concerned while getting to watch the first 3 games of the year in person. But there is an interesting footnote to add to the story.

Unlike most, if not all, of the people I have met since starting my first Huskers book in 2015, neither Michael nor Monica was born in Nebraska. Their only physical connection to the state is that Michael attended UNL for a couple of years in the late 90s, during which time he became a diehard Big Red fan. Meanwhile, Monica described herself as having been "converted by marriage" to the Cornhuskers Clan.

I can, of course, understand how Michael came to love the school and the state, and I can also relate to Monica's situation after having undergone the same matrimonial conversion experience myself.

This serves to underline a point that I have tried to make in my writing and in my personal interactions: namely that there is something special about the culture that surrounds the State of Nebraska and it's Big Red football program that is unique and appealing to people from places far beyond the state's borders. I have encountered a number of Nebraskans in my travels who dismiss the impact of the football program by saying "You've got to understand that we don't have anything else here besides the Huskers". Up until now, my counter has always been to say that although the internet makes Nebraskans freer than ever to follow any team in any sport anywhere around the world, I am always impressed that they choose to follow the Big Red.

This argument does not seem to make much of an impact, so perhaps I would do better to point out that although Michael, Monica and I were raised in different environments and have had plenty of other choices, we all now choose to follow the Huskers. Or better still, perhaps I should adapt the sentiments expressed on a bumper sticker that is commonly seen in Texas to make it read: "I wasn't born in Nebraska, but I became a Husker fan as soon as I could!"

As the game progressed, I had the privilege of meeting two of the senior alumni of the Californians for Nebraska club. Partway through the first quarter a distinguished elderly gentleman politely asked whether anyone was using the seat next to me. When I told him that the seat was free he sat down and seemed to enjoy the game and the friendly atmosphere in the bar, but after a while it became evident that he could not see the smaller details on the screen. He asked me the score from time to time, as well as the time on the clock, and during one of these exchanges I asked him about himself.

Ralph was born in 1932 and studied architecture at UNL before moving to California in 1960. He is originally from the town of Malcolm - which coincidentally is the town where Michael and Monica stayed during their recent Husker Three-peat - but he had spent most of his career in California designing high schools. I asked him whether he may have known my father-in-law Tom Hauser, who would have been just a few years behind him in the School of Architecture. Although Ralph did not recall that particular name, he enjoyed a chuckle when I told him how Tom had paid a fellow student to take the final Physics exam on his behalf so he could complete his degree on time.

My wife and I were also happy to meet Jodie, who is one of the founders of the Californians for Nebraska club. Originally from Kearney, Jodie was both lovely and elegant at the age of 90 dressed in her Huskers attire. Apart from being a loyal

Husker fan, Jodie is also a good sport who agreed to join me in singing the school fight song over the PA system at the bar after the Huskers' first touchdown of the second half. Jodie's favorite Huskers football memory is from early in 1998 when she happened to be in Miami overnight while on her way to take a long-planned cruise vacation.

The Orange Bowl was due to take place the night before her departure, and as luck would have it, the teams involved were Nebraska and Tennessee. Jodie was lucky indeed as this was to be an historic occasion since it was Tom Osborne's last game as Nebraska coach, and Peyton Manning's last game as Tennessee quarterback. Jodie's eyes twinkled as she chuckled while she recalled Tennessee fans leaving the game well before the finish, with Nebraska leading 35-9 early in the last quarter and going on to win 42-17.

This win clinched the national championship for Nebraska, and one can only imagine the spring in Jodie's step as she set off on her cruise the next day after having managed to be in the right place at the right time by sheer coincidence. No wonder it's her favorite Huskers memory!

May both Jodie and Ralph have many more happy Huskers memories to come.

CHAPTER FIVE

NUMBERS TELL THE TALE

With apologies to a certain television series of which I've heard but never actually seen, the 90,374 fans who filled Memorial Stadium for the contest against the Illinois Illini witnessed a Game of Threes. According to the Las Vegas bookmakers, the Huskers were favored to beat the Illini by three touchdowns. For the second week in a row, I did not believe

the bookies and for the second week in a row, I failed to put my money where my mouth was.

Apparently, the coaches and players from Illinois either did not read the papers during the week leading up to the game, or they simply chose to ignore the parts they didn't like - and in the midst of the ongoing election season, who could blame them? Either way, after a slow first quarter the Illini machine suddenly started firing on all cylinders and held a 13-10 lead at the half. Nebraska had dominated the time of possession in the first half and had gained more yards than the visitors, but the Huskers' momentum had stalled following an interception and a 56-yard field goal attempt by Drew Brown that fell short.

During the first half, Nebraska's three Heisman winners were introduced to the crowd, accompanied by a video highlight from each player commentated by the legendary Lyle Bremser. "Man, woman and child!" rang out through the stadium as we watched Rogers, Rozier and Crouch on screen zigzagging their way down the field to the end zone. The presence of those three famous players was most appropriate for this homecoming game, and at least one fan decided to mark the occasion by resurrecting a fashionable accessory from the

RETURN TO THE BIG RED ZONE · 67

Johnny Rogers era. Nothing makes a fashion statement quite like a fabulous red-and-white giant houndstooth plaid jacket.

The halftime break saw the crowning of the Homecoming King and Queen, Matthew Foley and Charlotte Sjulin, a pair of fine young students who have distinguished themselves with their achievements in the fields of academics, sport and community involvement.

Although I have never met Matt in person, he is the son of one of my wife Christi's friends from her undergraduate studies at Lincoln in the early 80s when she and Matt's mother Susan were Student Assistants in the Sandoz Residence Hall. Christi and Susan have managed to stay in touch through exchanging Christmas cards during the 30-plus years since their days of patrolling the residence hall floors and settling disputes among their fellow students over matters such as untidy roommates and messy bathrooms, and Christi had always spoken fondly of her fellow SA's. Thus, it was a vicarious pleasure for me to witness the continuation of Susan's family connection with the University.

So far, four of Susan's children have attended UNL, with two more waiting in the wings until they finish their high school education. After sending 6 children through the University of Nebraska system, Susan can probably be forgiven (even by diehard Big Red fans like my late father-in-law) for having married a man from out of state (New York, for crying out loud!).

This was the third Nebraska homecoming game since 2013 that featured Illinois as the visiting team, and while some fans had looked backward,

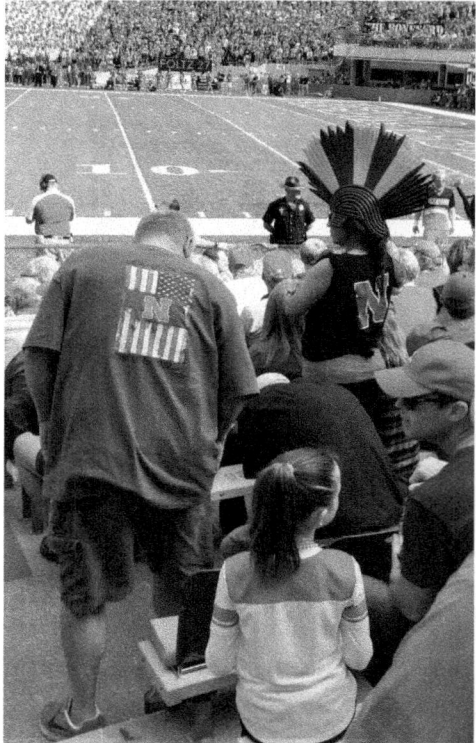

there were others who envisaged a whole different reality. We in the West Stadium were privileged to witness the presence of an Amazon goddess wearing her ceremonial red-and-black headdress while one of her subjects with an exotic flag design on his back bowed his head toward her in rapt homage.

In keeping with the Game of Threes theme, even the hot dog artillery got into the action by using their aptly-named "Wiener Schlinger" to launch three of their tempting treats into the sky above the crowd simultaneously instead of their usual solo shot. I had never seen them do this before, which only goes to demonstrate how thoroughly the day's governing theme of three had been communicated before the game throughout the ranks of the small army of vendors, sweepers, ushers and other employees that man the stores, stands and hallways of Memorial Stadium each week.

The number three was to rear its head again before the game ended, as that is exactly how many touchdowns Nebraska scored in the final quarter. Trailing 10-16 three minutes into the final stanza of the game, the Huskers finally awoke from their slumber with a 3-yard run from Terrell Newby that gave them the lead for good. Two more touchdowns sealed the 31-16 victory for the Huskers as they improved their record to 5-0.

Unfortunately, there was also a negative three during the game with Carter, Westerkamp and Ozigbo all sustaining injuries that took them out of the game. The only silver lining to this gloomy cloud was that the next week would be a bye for the Huskers, offering some extra recuperation time for these three important players.

At the press conference after the game, it was a very relieved Mike Riley who opened by asking the assembled media "Did you all stay around for the 4th quarter?" The room erupted in laughter, but there must have been some nervous coaches and players on the Nebraska sideline at the third quarter break when the Illini were holding on to a 16-10 lead over the 20-point favorite Huskers.

"I was really pleased with the way we fought back" Riley continued. "I have a lot of respect for Newby. He really stepped up today, and the line did a good job too."

Terrell Newby indeed had an outstanding day, rushing for 140 net yards during the game and two touchdowns in the 4th quarter.

In his usual manner, Riley also reflected on the things that hadn't gone according to plan, admitting that "I made a bad decision to try the long field goal. The wind was unpredictable." He said he was generally happy with the game, but noted there were still some areas to work on during the bye week.

For his part, Terrell Newby said he was very proud of the offensive line and that "I never get frustrated with the short runs like 3 or 4 yards, as long as we're moving the chains."

I almost wanted to tell him about the guy behind me in the crowd over my right shoulder who had yelled "Quarterback draw!" just before the snap on what seemed like every other Nebraska offensive play. Luckily for Newby and his team, it seemed that the Big Red coaches on the other side of the field were either not able to hear this tidbit of advice that was so stridently launched out in their direction, or else they chose to ignore it. The results spoke for themselves with Armstrong averaging 1.5 yards on his 8 carries for the day, and Newby averaging 5.2 yards on 27 carries.

In between the yells from behind me I had enjoyed talking with Michael, who was seated next to me and was probably a few years older than me. He and his wife Nancy spoke of their memories of listening to Husker games on the radio during their younger days, and like many youngsters growing up in the state, Michael always dreamed of playing for the Huskers. He eventually walked on as a player and said that his most unusual memory took place during the conditioning program the players were required to follow during the winter season.

Monte Kiffin was one of the assistant coaches at the time, and he would bring the players to a racquetball court where they would be divided into pairs. One person in each group of two would be handed a broomstick to hold with both hands, and it was the job of his partner to wrestle that broomstick away using any method that he saw fit. The only hard and fast rule to guide the ensuing mayhem was that kicks to the groin area were not allowed.

As I tried to visualize in my mind the picture of pairs of grappling, grunting bodies strewn all over a perfectly respectable racquetball court, I was suddenly distracted by a much more peaceful image. With just under 5 minutes left in the game, Tommy Armstrong had thrown a 6-yard pass to Trey Foster for a touchdown. But it was what happened after the extra point that caught my attention.

I had witnessed many times the crowd ritual for celebrating a touchdown, which always began with the fans waving their arms above their heads, swaying back and forth from the elbow while the band started to play "Dear Old Nebraska U". I had asked on a couple of occasions about the meaning of the waving arms, and the best answer I received was that it represented the waving of Nebraska cornfields. I must admit I failed to see the connection – how could waving arms look like a cornfield? Eventually, I gave up on the subject because the answers I was receiving made no sense in my antipodean mind

That is to say, it made no sense until late in the Illinois game when the sun was low in the sky behind me and the fans in the south-eastern corner of the stadium were bathed in a golden late-in-the-day light. Even though it was early October, the temperature had been in the upper 60s and most fans were wearing t-shirts or other short-sleeved tops.

As the band launched into their rendition and arms all around the stadium launched into the air, I glanced across the field and saw thousands of bare golden arms swaying rhythmically back and forth. To me, it looked just like a field of wheat with its stalks being buffeted gently to and fro by the wind. It created in my mind a peaceful rural vision in the midst of 90,000 people. "There is no place like Nebraska", continued the band. Indeed.

The Numbers Tell the Story

Following on from the discussion on the game of threes, some of the more outstanding figures from the matchup against Illinois provide further insight into how the game was won and lost.

72: The number of plays run by Nebraska during the game.

44: The number of plays run by Illinois.

38: The total minutes of possession during the game by the Huskers' offense.

11: The number of minutes consumed by the Huskers' 18-play drive that culminated in the go-ahead touchdown early in the fourth quarter.

21: The total number of points scored by Nebraska in the fourth quarter.

3: The number of possessions by Illinois during the fourth quarter, each of which resulted in a three-and-out.

114: The number of rushing yards gained by Nebraska during the fourth quarter.

113: The number of the above rushing yards gained by Terrell Newby.

Although these numbers are important on their own in the context of that particular game, they take on more significance when compared to the 2015 season.

5: The number of games the Huskers have won so far in the 2016 season. Also the total number of wins by the Huskers during the entire 2015 regular season.

2: The number of games the Huskers had won at this same point in the 2015 season.

4: The number of games lost by Nebraska in 2015 during the final minute of the game. (It still hurts.)

6: The total number of points scored against Nebraska during the first quarter of the 5 games played so far in 2016.

115: The total number of points scored against Nebraska during the first quarter of the 13 games played in 2015.

78: The total number of points scored by Nebraska during the fourth quarter of the 5 games played so far in 2016.

141: The total number of points scored by Nebraska during the fourth quarter of the 13 games played in 2015.

3: The number of penalties against Nebraska during the Illinois game.

13: The number of penalties against Nebraska in each of two games during 2015.

So, what do all these numbers mean (apart from the fact that I obviously have too much time on my hands)? The win-loss record on its own shows that the Huskers are headed for a much better season than the last one, but the other figures provide us with some insight into the reasons for the turnaround.

While the Huskers collapsed during the fourth quarter of many of their 2015 games, causing them to lose in some close finishes, in 2016 the situation has so far been reversed. We have seen the defense strangling the opposition and allowing the offense to spend more time on the field to reap the benefits of the physical onslaught they have mounted for the first three-quarters of the game. While I am in no position to know for certain, it seems to me that an improved conditioning program combined with an increased level of confidence in their coaches and team-mates is what has allowed the Huskers to run away from their opponents during the fourth quarter.

For example, when Terrell Newby was handed the ball during the closing minutes of the Illinois game with the lead at 24-16, no-one would have complained if he had simply run for a first down on his 16th carry of the quarter to set up further running plays to use up the clock. Instead, excellent blocking from his teammates opened up a hole for Newby who had the physical reserves to outsprint four defenders on a 63-yard dash to the end zone.

Another area of tangible improvement is evident in the decreased number of penalties assessed against the Huskers. During the 2015 season Coach Riley emphasized the need to improve this facet of the game, as it cost the team dearly on a number of occasions and made a material difference in tight games. The low number of Big Red penalties against Illinois allowed the score to remain close until the home team was able to take control during the fourth quarter.

While we all know that statistics can be manipulated to tell almost any kind of far-fetched story (and we are reminded of that fact almost daily during the current election season), the figures above point toward a much happier year for Husker fans than the last. I'm thinking of 10-2 but I won't be too upset if that first number ends up higher!

CHAPTER SIX

TOP TEN LIST

After starting the Illinois game ranked 15th overall in the nation, the Huskers were promoted 5 places to number 10 as they entered their next game. It had been 5 years since the Huskers were last in the top 10 in the national rankings, and there was no reason to think they shouldn't consolidate their spot over the next two weeks at least. Big Red fans were hoping for a much more positive outcome than that of 2011 when the Huskers spent a grand total of one week in the lofty company of the ten top teams in the country before going out the following week and losing to Northwestern.

Not that the coming game in Memorial Stadium could be expected to be easy, even though the Huskers would be playing on what sounds like their home turf. This particular Memorial Stadium is located in Bloomington, Indiana and the Huskers would be facing the 3-2 Hoosiers who beat Michigan State and gave second-ranked Ohio State a run for their money just a week earlier in Columbus. Just to add a little more spice to the pre-game chili, the Huskers were at risk at being without three of their most productive offensive weapons so far this season:

Ozigbo, Carter and Westerkamp. These Three Huskerteers
(well OK, it's really one plus
two. The other two need to get
working on their mustaches so
they can match the swashbuckling Westerkamp) had together
accounted for 10 touchdowns in
the past five games, and Ozigbo
had carried the ball a team-lead-
ing 76 times.

Meanwhile, the Husker de-
fense would likely have its work
cut out for it because after the first five games of the season the
Hoosiers were the Big 10 leaders in passing yardage at 293
yards per game, in comparison to the Huskers' 238 yards. On
the other hand, in the ground game the Huskers had averaged
4.9 yards per carry compared to 3.9 yards for the Hoosiers.

While this was to be the Huskers' first game against Indiana
since joining the Big 10, my wife and I would also be making
a debut of our own over the game weekend as we planned to
put Lily the mini huskerhound into the boarding kennel and
take the train up to San Francisco to watch the game in the company of the Bay Area Huskers. We were hoping that the
libations served by the Final Final Bar would provide sufficient
lubrication to encourage the Huskers faithful to sing "Dear Old
Nebraska U' with us after each touchdown. I would think that
the local fans would be no strangers to adult beverages since
they live so close to the Napa Valley where they make all of
those Nebraska-colored red and white wines.

The Bloomington weather for the game was predicted to be sunny and 76 degrees, so all was set for what looked to be an exciting contest. While Nebraska had started each of its games slowly so far this season before finishing strong, Husker fans were concerned that their lads may not have that same luxury of coming back from behind against the Hoosiers with its pass-heavy, quick scoring offense.

Coach Riley was likely thinking the same thing when he said during the week: "We have to remind [our guys] that it's not against the rules to score in the first and get something going."

Eureka in California

"Quarterback draw!" That was the first thing I heard when my wife and I walked into the Bay Area Huskers watch party halfway through the first quarter of the game against Indiana. The cozy space of the Final Final Bar was filled with 80 or so fans paying eager attention to the screens placed in all corners of the room, most of which were tuned to the Nebraska game. We had found our way to the prestigious Presidio Heights area of San Francisco where quaint two- and three-story homes priced north of $3 million dollars surrounded the old-style corner bar owned by a man whom we were variously told came from Lyons, NE or from western Nebraska. Given that Lyons is not far from Nebraska's eastern border, there is quite a difference between the two competing accounts of his hometown.

The grey-haired man in question was very busy behind the scenes throughout the day so I never got to ask him for myself, but nevertheless it felt like were in Lincoln where a couple of weeks ago I had heard another animated fan calling out the same play every few minutes or so. The only difference on this particular day was that there were a few fans sprinkled here and there who were trying to watch the Arizona State game, but these poor souls soon realized they were outnumbered and gradually drifted away to leave the Big Red faithful to their own devices.

As we looked around after taking out seats near the covered pool table, I could see that in true Nebraska style the crowd included fans of all ages from college students to retirees. Directly to our left were Jim and Shari who were visiting on vacation from Elwood, NE, and as we sat down we saw them enjoying a red beer as they intently watched the game.

This on its own was a clear indication that the owner of the establishment was from Nebraska, because where else in San Francisco could one walk up to the bar and order a red beer without batting an eyelid? I'm sure that in most other places the crush of the crowd, he soon found himself next to the now-horizontal goalpost. Then someone said: "Let's carry the goalpost to the State Capitol!" And so they picked up the goalpost.

But when they reached the steps of the stadium with their prize, they were met by a stern policeman with a bullhorn. "Put the goalpost down!" he said. And so they did.

But their fun was far from over as they left the stadium to continue their celebrations elsewhere. One can only wonder what might have happened if the goalpost had made it as far as the Capitol building. "Let's carry it up on to the roof!" might have been the next suggestion.

Turning my attention back to the game at hand, the Vols broke the stalemate by continuing to run the ball at will and by halfway through the quarter led the game 14-0. But the plucky Huskers fought back as Fyfe completed passes of 33 yards to Huskerteer Cethan Carter and 38 yards to Brandon Reilly Jr for their first touchdown of the day with 1.5 minutes left in the half. Most fans clapped along happily as I sang Dear Old Nebraska U, but as most often happens no-one knew the words. I think I need to make some giant cue cards with the words written in large block letters like they used to use on the Tonight Show and bring them with me next season. Either that, or not sing. But not singing would be no fun – I'd feel like an Ivy League fan for whom football is just a quaint little game and not a religion.

Not to be outdone by the Nebraska score, the Vols came back and moved the ball 75 yards in 9 plays to score their third touchdown just before the end of the first half.

Although the score was now 21-7, I had faith that the boys in red would fight back and so I turned my attention to the important matters of lunch and the half-time raffle.

Prime Rib Sandwich
Sliced Prime Rib topped with Lettuce and Tomato on toasted French Roll. Served with Au Jus (Horseradish upon request) $11.49

Jami's Special
Pastrami, Turkey and Bacon on Parmesan Cheese bread with lettuce and Thousand Island dressing. $10.29

Grilled Italian Sandwich (Hot & Spicy)
Beef Italian Sausage links on French Roll topped with Peppers and Onions, Jack Cheese. mustard. $1(

Italian Sub
Salami, Mortadella, Pepperoni, Provolone Cheese with Lettuce, Tomato, Red Onion, Pepperocinis and Ital dressing. $10.29

Monte Christo Sandwich
Turkey, Ham and Cheese breaded with Mayo in an Egg batter and deep fried. $10.99

I had planned to order a chicken sandwich but then I saw the Monte Christo Sandwich which sounded to me like a nice healthy turkey sandwich, lightly breaded. But instead of the low-fat low-calorie offering that I had imagined, Monte Christo turned out to be just as much of a mouthful as the name of the Bowl game the Huskers were engaged in.

This vision of clotted cholesterol resembled nothing so much as two pieces of enormously greasy French toast stuffed with ham and cheese along with some token slices of turkey, accompanied with an ample serving of French fries. Talk about eating first with my eyes – I could barely stand to look at the culinary creation in front of me. But just like the Huskers who were facing a considerable challenge in Nashville, I refused to let myself be defeated by the daunting task in front of me.

After consuming this heart attack on a plate and praying that the miracle of the coming New Year would magically bring a spontaneous loss of 5 pounds or more, I somehow managed to lift my lead-filled stomach off my chair to greet Ted who had won dual prizes in the half-time raffle. The first prize was a

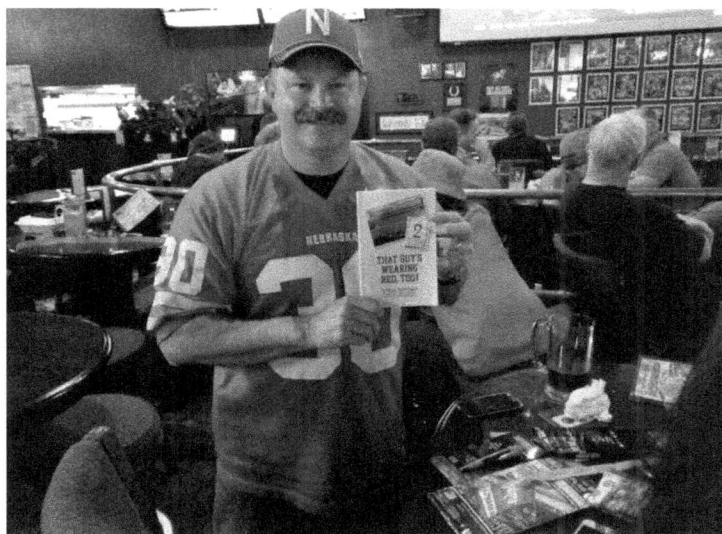

copy of my book on the 2015 Husker season "That Guy's Wearing Red, Too!", but the second prize was something that no self-respecting Husker fan should ever be without. It was a musical pen that played the school fight song. I didn't check to

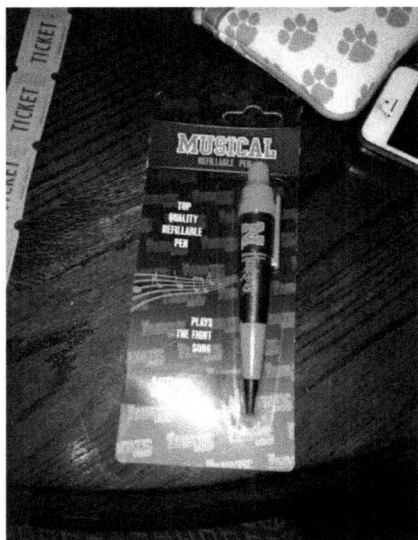

see whether the words were printed on the packaging but at least I know they are printed in the book, so I hope Ted will do his homework during the off-season and be ready to stand and sing with me in 2017. Meanwhile, I will spend my time imagining Ted proudly wearing his Big Red Pen in his top pocket and using it at every opportunity to sign checks, contracts and other important papers while the fight song plays bravely in the background.

The Huskers would have to make some adjustments at half-time and I hoped that none of them had eaten a Monte Christo during the break as they would need all of their wits about them to slow down the Vols' offense that had gained 140 yards through the air and 94 on the ground during the second quarter. Nebraska meanwhile had gained only 2 yards on 5 rushing attempts and 82 yards in passing plays.

Although Nebraska's first drive of the half was halted by a fumble after a completed pass, the Blackshirts managed to slow the Vols' offense down a little and restrict them to a single field goal for the quarter. For the Big Red, Husketerteer Devine Ozigbo's 42-yard rush was the key play in a 75-yard drive that resulted in a 9-yard Fyfe touchdown pass to Reilly Jr. With 15 minutes remaining in the game, the Huskers trailed 14-24 but would face the Vols on the Huskers' 10-yard line when play resumed.

It took just 4 plays of the final quarter for the Vols to drive the remaining 10 yards into the Huskers' end zone, despite the fervent hopes of the Big Red fans for a Tennessee fumble and a change of possession.

Another long completion by Fyfe of 39 yards to Reilly Jr was the highlight of the Huskers' next possession which ended in a 45-yard field goal by Drew Brown that brought the score to 17-31 with 12 minutes remaining in the game. On the ensuing kickoff, much to the delight of the crowd at Danny K's, the Huskers forced a fumble and regained the ball on the Vols' 31-yard line. Fyfe was more than up to the occasion to take advantage of the sudden changes of fortunes as he led a 5-play drive that culminated in a 9-yard run by the quarterback into the end zone to bring the score to 24-31 with 10 minutes to play.

The excitement in the room was palpable as the crowd sensed the possibility a courageous come-from-behind win by their never-say-die Huskers. But the Vols had other plans and took the ball 77 yards down the field in 4 plays to score a touchdown to bring the score to 38-24 in their favor and deflate the rising hopes of the Huskers faithful.

Even though some 8 minutes remained in the game, neither team was able to gain much further traction as they traded possessions and time ran out with a 14-point victory for the Tennessee Volunteers.

In the end, it was a fitting result because the Vols looked like the better team throughout the game with their 230 rushing yards compared to 61 by the Big Red. Nevertheless, the gritty Huskers were far from disgraced as they kept fighting back and drew within a touchdown during the fourth quarter after trailing by 17 points halfway through the third period. Huskerteer Ozigbo led the rushers with 66 yards and Fyfe threw for 243 yards and two touchdowns.

Although the season had not ended on the same high note as 2015 with a Bowl win, the Huskers had put up a good fight and could content themselves that at 9-4 their program had improved considerably during the past year.

CHAPTER FOURTEEN

LESSONS FOR NEXT YEAR

"Well, they might have been a bit overrated early in the season" said John, an expatriate Nebraskan now living in southern California. This seemed to be a common sentiment among sports pundits of various types as they reflected on the Huskers' 2016 campaign. It was hard to argue with that opinion when we look back at the 7-0 Huskers being ranked seventh in the nation before the Wisconsin game, prior to which the number 22 Oregon was the only team they had played against in the top 25. However, the Huskers proved that they really were up to the task against the number 11 Badgers and were unfortunate not to have won that pivotal game.

The voters in the national ranking polls saw it the same way, and the overtime loss to the Badgers only caused the then 7-1 Huskers to drop two places to ninth position. Although the critics were silenced to some degree by the Huskers' performance against the Badgers, the chorus of naysayers resumed with renewed vigor after the disappointing loss to Ohio State.

Judging by the polls, 2016 was indeed a dynamic season for the Big Red as they were initially unranked, burst into the top 25 after beating Oregon, and rose as high as seventh before gradually tumbling down to 24th position prior to their bowl game which pushed them back out of the top 25. Nevertheless, Husker fans must have been pleased by the team's resurgence following the disappointment of 2015. Although some fans were impatient to see the Huskers reclaim a steady position in the top 10, there would have been few who would not have been pleased prior to the first game of 2016 if they had known that the Big Red would be ranked in the top 25 for all but the first 3 games of the year and would finish the season with 9 wins.

Both Sam Hahn and Josh Banderas played significant roles in the Huskers' success, with the ND State transferee Hahn starting 9 games and receiving the honor of the Huskers' 2016 Walk-on of the Year. Meanwhile Banderas not only led the team as one of its four captains, but also led the team in tackles, recording a total of 93 from his position as middle linebacker.

Although my experience with the Huskers only began some 16 years ago, I have noted some significant changes during that period to the Big Red football program beginning with the firing of Frank Solich. As a fan of the team for more than 70 years, my late father-in-law Tom Hauser grew up watching the Huskers pound the rock and for him the pinnacle of the game was to watch a running back step through a hole in the defense and make what he would gleefully pronounce to be a "beautiful run". The hiring of Bill Callahan with its emphasis on the passing game was thus very difficult for Tom to watch, as the team and organization struggled with the radical change to its approach on offense. Prior to his passing away, Tom was very happy to see the return to a more run-centric approach under the leadership of Bo Pelini.

But of course, no matter what type of offensive scheme any team uses, it all comes down to the quarterback to execute the plans of the coaching staff. Winding the clock forward a few years from the Callahan years, Tommy Armstrong was indeed the right quarterback to straddle both sides of the run vs. pass debate. Not only could he drop back and pass, he was also very mobile and elusive in his rushing with the ball and went on to set numerous Nebraska records. He clearly enjoyed playing for the Huskers and put everything he had into each game – often to his own physical detriment. It was sometimes difficult to watch him at the post-game press conference when he would walk slowly and gingerly to the podium, careful not to further aggravate his latest injuries, strains or bruises.

As a fan, I was happy to watch Tommy zig-zag down the field as he sidestepped would-be tacklers and advanced the ball towards – and often over – the goal line. But as a writer and observer, I often wondered about the source of his motivation to keep going week after week. I figured that he was probably aware that he would be regarded as too small to play quarterback at the next level, and there were plenty of running backs who would present a more impressive résumé to NFL talent scouts than he would. In my mind, therefore, I had concluded that Tommy had realized that his college career with Nebraska would be his one and only chance of fulfilling his lifelong dream of playing competitive football. Given all that, I certainly salute his courage because I can't help but wonder what it must have felt like when he slowly dragged himself up off the ground after being pancaked by 300-pound linebackers for the umpteenth time each game. It must have been very hard in such moments to sit back and think "Gee, these are the best years of my life!"

But coming back to the eternal run vs. pass debate, statistics from the 6-7 2015 season showed that the Huskers were much more successful when they ran more rushing plays than passing. Just to summarize, the 2015 Huskers averaged 1.6 run plays for every pass attempt during the games that they won. On the other hand, during games that they lost the Huskers ran 0.9 run plays for every pass attempt.

Applying the same analysis to the 9-4 2016 season yields strikingly similar results:

- During the 9 games that they won, the Huskers averaged 1.7 run plays for every pass attempt.
- During their 4 losses, the Huskers ran 0.9 run plays for every pass attempt.
- The significance of this run/pass ratio is emphasized by the Wisconsin game which the Huskers almost won and which at 1.4 had the highest value for a losing game.
- The ratio in the other three losing games was 0.7, 0.8 and 0.7.

Lovers of the running game such as my late father-in-law would happily conclude from the above that the Huskers should return to the run-first approach that was so successful in the team's glory years. It will be interesting to see what type of quarterback leads the offense during the 2017 season, and whether he has the dual-threat capability that Armstrong and some of his predecessors brought to the program.

No matter who is under center, Husker fans will hope that the encouraging upward trajectory of their Big Red boys will continue into 2017 and beyond.

Speaking of Husker fans, if I were to compare the attitudes and reactions of the red-clad supporters I met in 2015 compared to those I met in 2016, I would conclude that there was very little difference between the 6-7 fans of 2015 and the 9-4 fans of 2016. While the 2015 fans continued to hope for better days and more consistency in the program, there was a sense of gracious humility among many of the 2016 fans. Although the latter group was pleased by the Huskers' winning streak to start the season, at the same time they seemed also a little embarrassed by the attention the program attracted. Rather than loudly bragging that the Big Red was "back", they took it all in stride and modestly preferred to let the team's results speak for themselves.

Of course they did – they're Nebraskans. I shouldn't have expected anything less from the greatest fans in college football. Long may they and their program prosper – including especially Mike and Jen's newborn little Husker fan who will be able to join his sisters at the family tailgate next year.

APPENDIX

SEASON RESULTS

2016 Nebraska Cornhuskers

Date	Opponent	Result	Record	AP Rank
Sep. 3	Fresno State	W 43-10	1-0	-
Sep. 10	Wyoming	W 52-17	2-0	-
Sep. 17	Oregon (22)	W 35-32	3-0	-
Sep. 24	@Northwestern	W 24-13	4-0	20
Oct. 1	Illinois	W 31-16	5-0	15
Oct. 15	@Indiana	W 27-22	6-0	10
Oct. 22	Purdue	W 27-14	7-0	8
Oct. 29	@Wisconsin (11)	L 17-23	7-1	7
Nov. 5	@Ohio State (6)	L 62-3	7-2	9
Nov. 12	Minnesota	W 24-17	8-2	21
Nov. 19	Maryland	W 28-7	9-2	19
Nov. 25	@Iowa	L 10-40	9-3	17
Dec. 30	Tennessee	L 24-38	9-4	24

ABOUT THE AUTHOR

Steve Banner spent most of his working career in adult
education in the telecommunications industry before changing
his path to tax and accounting, and then finally branching out
part-time into his longed-for field of travel writing. He counts
himself blessed to have two wonderful children and to be
married to his very supportive and ever-patient Nebraskan
wife.

reaction from the barman would range somewhere between "Please explain" and "Throw this weirdo out".

And once again in true Nebraska style, after we got talking with Jim he invited us to join him at his pre-game tailgate next week in Lincoln. It seems that he has the whole tailgate routine honed down to a fine art as he works his Husker Hospitality out of a trailer that he keeps stored in Lincoln, and which he delivers to his regular spot on Friday evening and retrieves on Sunday while overnighting in between in a nearby condo.

A group of college-age students was to our right, and they too were enjoying the game, but being of a certain age they did not bother with putting tomato juice in their glasses and thereby wasting space that could be far more gainfully occupied by beer. Before long another of their friends arrived, and after being greeted all around she was quickly supplied with a red t-shirt that one of the well-prepared members of the group had brought along in case of an emergency such as a friend arriving without one of the indispensable accessories for game-watching.

This particular shirt was labeled "Nashville Huskers", and after quickly donning it the new arrival blended into the crowd of red shirts around the room. Just a few minutes later the room erupted when Chris Jones intercepted an errant Hoosiers pass and ran it back for a Huskers touchdown. After waiting for the extra point, I waited to see if the owners of the bar were going to play the fight song. When nothing of the kind happened, I took a deep breath and launched into singing "Dear Old Nebraska U".

As you know all too well by now, dear readers, I have spent many lonely moments singing the fight song at the top of my lungs, as the solitary voice while surrounded by red-clad Nebraska fans. If ever you have wondered what if feels like to be all alone in a crowd then this is a surefire way to find out. To put it on a more topical note, just imagine if you will being at a rally for Hillary Clinton and then standing up and yelling out "Trump for President!" But worse still, imagine standing up at the same rally and yelling "Hillary for President!" only to find that everyone ignores you.

And so it was with deep trepidation that I began to clap and sing. Maybe it was the joy of the unexpected touchdown, or perhaps the sophistication of the San Francisco crowd, or the red and non-red beer, but whatever the reason people all around me joined in with the clapping and several of them even sang along! I felt like Edison must have done when he discovered how to make the first successful light bulb. When asked about his thousands of failed attempts, he refused to be discouraged and replied: "I have not failed – I have so far discovered thousands of ways that the light bulb will *not* work". As for me, up until Saturday, I had discovered lots of places where Nebraska fans will *not* sing the fight song, and thus the precious "Eureka" moment at Final Final was all the more special.

If only the venerable deans at the University of Nebraska would see their way clear to include learning the words of the fight song in the core curriculum, the gleeful army of Big Red fans would surely impress their opponents all over the country as they sang about their fairest girls and squarest boys!

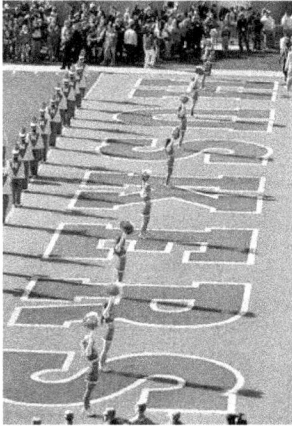

There is no place like Nebraska,
Dear old Nebraska U.
Where the girls are the fairest,
The boys are the squarest,
Of any old school that I knew!
There is no place like Nebraska,
Where they're all true blue.
We'll all stick together,
In all kinds of weather,
For dear old Nebraska U!

Temporarily Missing in Action

After an outstanding first quarter against Indiana in which they scored 17 unanswered points, the Huskers' offense was far less effective during the second and third quarters of the game – much to the dismay of the attentive crowd watching the game at the Final Final Bar. With Ozigbo limited by injury to one carry on the day, and in the absence of the other two Huskerteers Westerkamp and Carter, it was always going to be difficult to maintain an intense tempo on offense. But in line with the old saying that when one door closes, another one opens, the temporary downturn by the offense provided the opportunity for the Blackshirts to show what they could do. The defense was indeed up to the task as they held the quick-moving Hoosier offense to below average yardage in passing and rushing, while forcing 6 punts and recording 3 sacks.

However, by the time the final quarter began, the Huskers' offense had failed to build on its early advantage and the Big Red only led by two points as the score stood at 17-15. While Armstrong had shown flashes of brilliance at quarterback, he had also thrown two interceptions by this time and had completed only 8 of his 22 pass attempts.

The mood at the watch party was tense five minutes into the final quarter as Armstrong dropped back to pass and looked for receiver Stanley Morgan who had separated himself downfield from several defenders. Suddenly the room erupted as Morgan caught Armstrong's pass and nimbly sidestepped in almost the same motion, resulting in three Hoosier defenders colliding with one another like bumbling Keystone Kops and freeing Morgan to sprint untouched to the end zone for a 72-yard touchdown.

The joyous singing of the fight song that followed the extra point was tinged with relief as the margin had now extended into much safer territory. But it wasn't long before the tension returned to the room as the Hoosiers responded with a touchdown of their own to bring the score to 24-22 with 8:26 remaining to play.

On the ensuing possession, the reawakened Huskers' offense slowly and methodically progressed down the field while they used up the clock. However, the drive stalled at the Indiana 48-yard line where the Huskers faced 4th and 1. After quickly talking it over, the decision was made by Head Coach Riley in a demonstration of his faith in his players to go for the first down. Armstrong kept the ball on the next play and was soon lost in the melee of bodies piled on the ground while Big Red fans all across the country held their collective breath. After the referees had succeeded in untangling the mass of arms and legs, a measurement showed that Armstrong had indeed made the first down and we all sighed in relief. Even Lily the mini husk-erhound must have been relieved as she watched the game at her boarding kennel in Los Angeles.

Thanks to that critical play, the Huskers were able to continue their drive and eventually got within field goal range. But with 1:45 remaining, Newby was stripped of the ball on the Hoosiers 20-yard line, resulting in a fumble. The play was reviewed by the officiating crew while blood pressure soared among Husker fans across the country, and nerve-stead-ying shots of liquor were ordered at the bar in San Francisco. Fortunately for cardiac emergency rooms all over Nebraska, the ruling was overturned and the Huskers kept the ball within field goal distance.

Finally, with 45 seconds left in the game, Drew Brown came out to attempt the 39-yard kick but was halted in mid-stride when Nebraska called a timeout. I wasn't sure if Riley was try-ing to ice his own kicker, but Brown was unfazed by the delay and eventually split the uprights to extend the lead and make the score 27-22. The game was sealed when Williams inter-cepted a pass on the second play of the Hoosiers' desperate attempt to drive 75 yards in the final 45 seconds of the game.

After the final whistle, I had the pleasure of meeting a pair of the college-age fans who had watched and cheered for the

Huskers throughout the game. It turned out that Torie and Shelby are both from San Francisco and had graduated from the University of Nebraska earlier this year. The pair had been friends at high school, and when considering their choices for college they had agreed they wanted to attend a school with solid academic programs, a Greek system and the opportunity to participate in "the football experience".

It seems they were at least partly influenced in their final decision by Torie's brother-in-law who had attended Nebraska and spoke highly of the experience. So now here they were back in San Francisco, enjoying the game while surrounded by expatriate Nebraskans, visiting Nebraskans, and converted Nebraskans like myself - in other words, the adopted family in which they will always be welcome members.

And at 6-0, it's a very *happy* family right now!

CHAPTER SEVEN

EXERCISE VS EXORCISE

What a difference one letter makes.

And what a difference one year makes.

At this same time in 2015, the Huskers owned a rather melancholy 2-4 win-loss record as they prepared for their seventh game of the season. Several weeks later the melancholy mood would turn to full-blown clinical depression when the Huskers lost 45-55 against the perennial basement-dwellers Purdue, creating a 3-6 record by that point of the year as the team struggled to adjust to coaches who approached the game in a manner that was almost diametrically opposed to that of their predecessors on the sidelines in Lincoln.

But since those dark and dismal days of 2015. the ensuing 180-degree turnaround had been nothing short of remarkable as the Huskers would bring a 6-0 record and a number 8 national ranking into their home game against Purdue. In fairness, both Nebraska players and coaches would say that their adjustment to one another's ideas and capabilities was not yet 100 percent complete, but any impartial observer would agree that the process has progressed well and has built upon the enormous strides that were made in the latter part of the prior year after the Huskers hit rock bottom away from home against the Boilermakers.

Many readers may recall, and I personally will never forget, that in the very next game after that painful loss in West Lafayette, IN, the Huskers came out and beat the highly-fancied and highly-ranked Michigan State Spartans in a thrilling game in Lincoln. Given the respective performances of the Huskers (6-0) and the Boilermakers (3-3) up to this point of the 2016 season, it was fair to say that the game was likely to result in a resounding win for the Huskers, who were 24-point favorites.

But more importantly, I hoped that history would repeat itself to the extent that the Purdue game would be a springboard that would allow the Big Red to come out the next week against a highly-ranked opponent in Wisconsin and show a national TV audience what they are really capable of doing.

In my mind, the Purdue game would allow the Huskers to exorcise their horrific memories of last year, while at the same time setting up the opportunity for the following week to exercise their game plan against the highly-fancied Badgers and reap the rewards of many months of planning and training.

The Boilermakers were in something of a state of disarray going into the Nebraska game, having fired their Head Coach a few days earlier after losing to Iowa by two touchdowns. After receiving the bad news halfway through his fourth season at Purdue, it must have been tempting for the poor chap to console himself by downing a few Boilermakers of his own.

Broken Records and Slow Learners

The game certainly began good style – so I was told – because I missed the first few minutes while making my way around to my seat in the East Stadium. Kieron Williams had intercepted an errant pass on Purdue's first play of the game from scrimmage, giving the Huskers the ball on the Boilermak-

ers' 22-yard line. Armstrong's running touchdown on the next play (which took place 16 seconds into the game) was not a bad way to kick things off for the home team, and I'm sure many of us thought that this would be the pattern of the day as the Huskers marched on towards beating the 24-point spread against lowly Purdue. However, just as we had seen in the prior week's game against the Hoosiers, the Boilermakers had other ideas, made the Big Red fight for every point, and in fact led the game 14-10 at the halftime break.

Thanks to the ever-reliable ticket man Bob who always seems to be prepared with a diverse supply of game tickets, I have the pleasure of sitting in a different part of the stadium for each game. This not only allows me to continually meet new people, but it also allows me to enjoy the benefit of experiencing the game from their perspective.

My seat for the Purdue game was next to Mike, who was visiting from southern California with his family. Mike's daughter is a student at UNL, and he and his wife were not only visiting her but also giving their high school senior son the opportunity to look around the UNL campus for himself. Mike has coached football for the past 11 years in a Pop Warner league in California, but unfortunately the timing of this family visit coincided with the final game of Mike's team which had been undefeated up until that point of the season. But thanks to the wonders of the wireless world, Mike was able to stay in touch with his fellow coaches on the other side of the country and receive regular updates to inform him that his team was up to the task of playing without him and would eventually manage to preserve their unbeaten season.

Even though he was 1,500 miles away from his own team, I was intrigued to hear Mike's coaching instincts bubbling to the surface from time to time throughout the Nebraska game as he offered unsolicited verbal advice to the Huskers from across the stadium. While he and I both had the same elevated vantage point to watch the game, his trained eye saw far more than mine.

There were a number of times when I wished I had a DVR at my fingertips so that I could replay each down in slow motion and let him talk me through the intricacies of individual plays where he talked of holes that rushers had missed, or cornerbacks that had played too far off their receivers. By happy coincidence, Mike lives not far from me in Orange County, so I hoped we might get the chance to meet a week later at the Californians for Nebraska watch site at the OC Tavern, in which case I'd be able to continue my education.

Although I did not grow up watching American football, I was pleased to learn that I was not the only Aussie in the crowd for the Purdue game. I had accepted the kind invitation of Jim and Shari, whom my wife and I had met a week earlier in San Francisco, to attend their pre-game tailgate outside the stadium and after making sure I was comfortably supplied with food and drink, Jim introduced me to Chris and Kris, an Australian couple who was visiting from Houston.

During the course of our conversation I learned that up until recently, these two antipodeans with almost-interchangeable names had owned and operated a winery in the Sonoma area of California. It all began when the couple had been living in the Phoenix area for several years, and they learned of a 56-acre vineyard and winery that was for sale. I can imagine that the thought of leaving the desert of Arizona in favor of the temperate regions of Northern California must have seemed very appealing, and so the decision to change careers and locations was made accordingly. After running the operation for 15 years or so, the couple eventually sold the property and relocated to Houston.

I didn't dare inquire as to their motivation to move eastwards – perhaps they were tired of all the beautiful scenery and fresh air in the countryside, and they longed for perpetual views of oil refineries on the horizon interrupted only by the occasional hurricane. But rather than talk about geography, we talked about football.

Chris had played Aussie Rules football at the highest level in Melbourne, so I'm sure that like me he had at first wondered why these Yanks run around throwing the ball to one another instead of kicking it. (Why do they even call the game "football" when the ball so rarely touches anyone's foot?) Their lovely daughter Elise who was raised in the US may have been able to explain it to them, but we who have reached a certain age need teachers with the patience of guys like Mike who are used to dealing with slower and more childish minds.

But even with all of his knowledge of football, Mike himself received an education of sorts at Memorial Stadium. He had received his college education at USC and had been to many of their games over the years, but this was his first Nebraska game. As he said several times throughout the course of the game "I have never seen an atmosphere like this."

Welcome to the club, Mike. Now you know why I was inspired to write a book and blog this season and last. Even though I was once again a lonely soul singing the words of the fight song during the game, there truly is no place like Nebraska.

And for a while during the game, it looked like there was no offense in Nebraska either. After kicking a field goal with 4 minutes left in the first quarter to make the score 10-7 in their favor, the heavily-favored Huskers did not score again until halfway through the third quarter. In the interim, they had 5 possessions during which they ran 21 plays for a total of 94 yards, including 4 punts and an interception. However, on their 6th possession since their last score, the Huskers finally put together a 5-play drive that culminated in spectacular fashion with a 40-yard touchdown pass to Pierson-El on a slant route.

It had been a clear sunny day with the stadium filled to colorful capacity, and Armstrong's pass to Pierson-El was just picture perfect as it hit him in stride, right on the chest.

This seemed to be just the spark the offense needed to wake it from its slumber, as on its next possession it strung together an 11-play drive for 82 yards capped off by a 24-yard rushing touchdown from Alonzo Moore. With 14 minutes left in the game, the Huskers led 24-14, with plenty of time left to score another touchdown or two. However, those brave souls who had bet on Nebraska were disappointed, because although the Huskers had three further possessions in the 4th quarter all they could manage was two field goal attempts, of which only one was good. The boys in red had run 21 plays for a total of 114 yards in these three final drives, but they also committed 5 penalties during the three series which set them back 50 yards in total. Ironically enough, the Huskers had only committed two penalties in the first three-quarters of the game,

Reflecting on the 27-14 final score at the post-game press conference, Coach Riley began by apologizing for sounding like a broken record when he said that he was happy for the win, even though the team had not played as well as he would have liked. He expressed his sentiments by saying "We expect to look better than that, and play better than that."

Speaking for myself as someone who witnessed his press conferences through the dark days of the 2015 season where Riley frequently apologized for his team letting the game get away from them, I must say I much prefer the 2016 version of Riley's broken record. A national top 10 ranking and a 7-0 record is music to my ears after the discordant mess that found the Huskers with a 3-4 record at this same time last year.

And what better way to celebrate the current state of the Huskers' record than treat myself to a corn-fed Nebraska Whisky Ribeye Steak from Cascio's in Omaha? The long, hungry drive back from Lincoln was well worth the effort but in my unthinking haste to order a drink prior to my celebratory feast I ordered a glass of cabernet. A Boilermaker would have been the perfect choice for the occasion!

Boilermaker Drink*

Ingredients
1-ounce whiskey
Beer
Shot glass
Beer glass

Method
Fill the shot glass with whiskey and place upright in the bottom of the empty beer glass. Fill the remainder of the beer glass with beer.

*Back in the 1930s this drink was also known as a Block and Fall, because of a popular saying associated with it: "Drink two, walk a block and fall."

CHAPTER EIGHT

HEEEERE'S NORFOLK!

Sunday morning following a Huskers home game usually finds me arising before dawn in Omaha to catch my flight back to my home in California. Normally I'm happy at the prospect of returning home, but I would have been pleased to make an exception for the weekend of the Purdue game. I would have liked to have stayed one more day in Nebraska to honor the memory of a man who was raised in the state and brought happiness and laughter into millions of lives during his professional career.

I am referring to the great Johnny Carson, whose 91st birthday fell on the Sunday after the Purdue game. Although he was born in Iowa, from the age of eight Johnny was raised in the charming town of Norfolk, where he is immortalized in an enormous mural painted on the wall of one of the buildings in the main downtown street West Norfolk Avenue, not far from Johnny Carson Boulevard and the Johnny Carson Theater.

According to the Norfolk Daily News, a birthday party was

planned for Carson the day after the Purdue game and according to a radio ad for the event that I heard, the highlight would be two hours of video clips from throughout the great man's career. Quite a compliment indeed to the man; a gathering to celebrate his life some years after his passing. While many would say that Johnny Carson remains revered because of his long career in entertainment which included 30 years as host of the Tonight Show, we Husker fans know that his true distinction lies in the fact that he graduated from the University of Nebraska in Lincoln.

Along with the ubiquitous reminders of Norfolk's favorite son, I was also captivated by the charm of the town's tree-lined main street with its well-preserved historic buildings and pedestrian-friendly ambiance. Beyond those obvious aesthetic charms, what really caught my eye was the impressively diverse range of businesses that operated on both sides of the street.

Unlike many towns that I had visited during the past year - which seemed to contain mostly bars, cafes and the occasional clothing store - during a short stroll along West Norfolk Avenue I found Main Street Bookstore, a bike shop, car tire dealer, children's clothing store, several banks, a couple of dance stu-

dios, a bridal shop and a pet store. This, of course, was in addition to a range of restaurants, cafes and bars. Obviously, I can't speak for the merchants and 25,000 residents of Norfolk, but the broad range of businesses combined with a large number of cars parked along the well-maintained street seemed to suggest a prosperous and thriving business environment.

I don't know how often the town's favorite son made it back to Norfolk before he died, but I'm sure he would be pleased to see what it has become.

Carson, of course, displayed no signs of nervousness as he hosted his show, and always seemed relaxed and at ease with his guests. A few days after leaving Norfolk I found myself wishing that I had his ability to cope effortlessly with stressful situations.

To put it in a nutshell, I developed a bad case of nervous anxiety when I heard that the winner of the Nobel Prize for Literature was to be announced a few days hence, and rumor had it that the award would go to an unconventional writer outside of the general literary mainstream.

The next few days were just a blur as I practiced my surprised look in the mirror, composed my acceptance speech and worked on the guest lists for the receptions in my honor at the Australian Embassy in Stockholm and the State Capitol in Lincoln. Well, dear reader as you have probably heard by now, the prize went to a certain Robert Zimmerman who is some obscure songwriter born in Minnesota of all places, and who apparently goes by the stage name of Bob Dylan. It's probably just as well I didn't win this year because it would have caused all kinds of problems in Hollywood when Hugh Jackman and Nicole Kidman canceled their movie shooting plans to fly to Stockholm to see me accept the award. Never fear, I've given them both advance notice to keep their schedules clear for this time next year. Oh, that reminds me, I must call Mel Gibson.

Seven-Eleven Saturday

Coming back to the matter at hand, the day finally arrived when the Huskers would face the first of their toughest tests of the season when they traveled to Madison to take on the Wisconsin Badgers. A win over the Badgers would surely give the Huskers a boost in confidence to take on Ohio State the following week.

With the Huskers ranked number 7 in the polls and the Badgers number 11, the game had garnered considerable national attention. Questions had been asked in the media for the previous few weeks while the Huskers climbed steadily upwards in the national rankings, about whether the lads from Lincoln truly deserved their elevated place on the ladder. Some Nebraska fans were outraged when the talking heads on ESPN snickered and raised the same question, seemingly regarding the Huskers as being overrated. Two weeks later on the day of the Wisconsin game, those same ESPN talking heads were serious indeed and split their votes 50/50 on which team would win.

Talking with Husker fans before the Purdue game, there was a strong belief that the Huskers would beat Wisconsin but would struggle with Ohio State the following week. But on the same day that the Huskers were dealing with Purdue, the once-invincible Buckeyes were shown by Penn State to have feet of clay as the Nittany Lions beat Ohio State 24-21 in Happy Valley.

It seemed to many observers that so far this season the Huskers had played only as well as they needed to each week, spending long periods of the game in neutral before shifting gears to finish off their opponents in the last quarter. We had seen signs of this same phenomenon last season when the Huskers lost to several unheralded teams but then played their best against the strong opposition of Michigan State and UCLA.

The Wisconsin game was thus set up to be a true test for the Huskers, and fortunately, the leader of the Three Huskerteers would be back in action with flowing mustache front and center. It was widely believed that Westerkamp's return would

boost the confidence of his teammates, especially Tommy Armstrong for whom he was a favorite target. Few of us will ever forget the key receptions that Westerkamp made last season during the game-winning last-minute drive to upset Michigan State. Just like the Badgers game, the Spartans game was played at night. Would we see history repeat itself with Westerkamp as the swashbuckling hero?

This was among the many questions in our minds as my wife and I drove to the Californians for Nebraska watch site at the OC Tavern in San Clemente.

As we pulled into the parking lot we commented that this quaint seaside town with its ocean pier could not be further from Nebraska in distance or ambiance, but as soon as we walked into the building we were immediately transported halfway across the country to the heartland of Nebraska. The first room we entered contained a wrap-around bar lined with stools, supplemented by tables scattered around the edges of the room. Most seats were occupied by red-shirted individuals with their gaze fixed on the nearest television screen.

We moved on to the second room, equal in size to the first, but with its walls lined with booth tables and the middle of the room filled with free-standing tables. A number of Husker fans had already arrived but there was room for us to secure a booth where we could await our new-found friends Gary and Dot.

My wife's sister Jenny had met Gary's and Dot's son Spencer a couple of weeks earlier when he came to her door in Orange County and introduced himself in his capacity as a realtor working in the area. Jenny and her family were not planning to sell their home but nevertheless she invited him inside to show him around. It didn't take long for the Nebraska "secret handshake" to take effect because Jenny soon found out that although Spencer had lived in California for 8 years, he was originally from Holdrege. He also informed her that just 6 weeks earlier his parents Gary and Dot had relocated to California to join him.

It wasn't long before Spencer and his parents arrived at the OC Tavern and we all settled in to watch the game. I gave them a copy of "That Guy's Wearing Red, Too!" but managed to hold my modesty in check and didn't tell them that it had almost won me a Nobel Prize a few days earlier.

Only one thing was certain as the game got underway: we could expect that a team wearing red and white would win. But not only did the teams wear the same colors, but they matched one another blow-for-blow on the field. The Badgers scored the first touchdown, but early in the second quarter Ozigbo ran for a 1-yard touchdown shortly after a 36-yard reception by fellow Huskerteer Westerkamp that took the ball to the Wisconsin 3-yard line. Around 10 or so of the 40 Husker fans in the room joined in as best they could with the fight song, with some singing and others clapping along while still others looked on with bemused puzzlement as they probably wondered how a Husker fan could possibly be "true blue" while clad from head to toe in red.

Armstrong struggled in the first half, completing just 4 of his 13 pass attempts and throwing two interceptions. The Nebraska defense, however, proved themselves up to the challenge and allowed the Badgers to score only three points from the visiting quarterback's miscues.

Halfway through the third quarter, the Badgers extended their lead to 17-7 and looked like the better team, even though the Huskers had outgained them in rushing yards during the first half. But continuing a pattern we had witnessed in previous games, the Huskers' offense finally hit its stride and put together a fourteen-play drive for a touchdown to reduce the deficit to 14-17 early in the final quarter. A key interception by Nate Gerry then gave the ball back to the Huskers at their own 30-yard line, leading to an 11-play drive that resulted in a 35-yard field goal from the ever-reliable Drew Brown to tie the score at 17-17.

The Badgers took over the ball with 3 minutes and 43 seconds left in the game and marched down the field until the drive stalled and the field goal kicker lined up for a 40-yard attempt to break the tied score. Much to the relief of the Husker fans at OC Tavern and all over the country, the kick sailed wide left of the uprights and the Huskers' offense ran on to the field with 1 minute 43 seconds left in front of a crowd of 80,833 full-throated fans roaring in the night.

Starting on the Huskers' own 27-yard line, Armstong threw two quick completions to Stanley Morgan and moved the ball to midfield while Brown warmed up on the sideline in anticipation of an opportunity to win the game off his boot. Even though the Huskers still had 2 time-outs remaining, they did not use them and instead the offense ran three hurried passing plays for no gain as the clock ticked down to 8 seconds left and they punted the ball away. I wanted to yell at the coaches through the TV that time-outs don't carry forward from one game to the next. They're not something you can keep in your back pocket and spend next week like a gift card with a credit balance!

Although Wisconsin had first possession of the ball in overtime, the Badgers left the door open for Nebraska to win the game. After scoring a touchdown, the Badgers missed the extra point so that the Huskers took over with the score at 17-23. A touchdown and extra point by the visitors would win the game and take the Huskers' unbeaten record into the next game against the highly-rated Ohio State.

Starting on the Badgers' 25-yard line and needing a touchdown for the win, the Huskers' first play was a 3-yard rush by Terrell Newby. The same player was handed the ball on the next play but was quickly stuffed by the Badgers' defense and lost a yard. The next play on 3rd and 8 was a pass attempt that fell incomplete. Amid the roaring of the crowd, the do-or-die pass attempt on 4th and 8 also fell incomplete, and suddenly the game was over.

Nebraska had lost its first game of the season but was far from disgraced. In many ways it was a warm-up for the big game next week, once again away from home, and once again it offered a chance for the Huskers to test themselves against the best in the land.

CHAPTER NINE

FLIPPING THE 6-9

For the second week in a row, the Huskers were to face a formidable opponent ranked within several rungs of them on the national ladder. After dropping only a couple of spots following their narrow loss in the 7-11 battle with Wisconsin, the Big Red lads would face another David and Goliath battle when they would take on Ohio State in a 6 versus 9 matchup.

Husker fans had long been nervously eyeing this game, and the one before it, ever since the schedule was released. Playing the Badgers and the Buckeyes away from home was always going to be a challenge, and I must admit that your Aussie Husker Fan had long ago mentally conceded both games in addition to the earlier matchup against Oregon. Had I known that the Huskers would be ranked 7th nationally going into the Wisconsin game and 9th leading into the Ohio State game I would likely have been much more optimistic.

Looking back on the Oregon and Wisconsin games, I must say I have never been happier to be wrong. The Huskers beat the Ducks in a tight and thrilling game while I watched on TV from the other side of the state in Scottsbluff, and six weeks later they had a golden opportunity to defeat the Badgers, only to see it slip agonizingly out of their reach.

But what we fans saw in the game against the Badgers was that the Huskers are a better team than they think they are. We have all seen cases in sport and in life where individuals or teams have an inflated opinion of themselves. While this over-confidence may give them a boost in courage as they face the challenges before them, the dangerously fragile foundation of that courage is quickly exposed when times get tough.

For example, on several occasions I have witnessed verbal displays of such misplaced overconfidence when flying into Las Vegas for a conference alongside holidaymakers who are planning to make sufficient money on the gambling tables to fund their extravagant vacation plans. I'm glad to say I have not been on hand to witness the subsequent reality check for these individuals when the mathematical forces arrayed against them inevitably caused their self-built houses of cards to come crashing down around them.

The Huskers on the other hand were, I believe, taken by surprise when the opportunity presented itself to win the Wisconsin game in overtime. But that opportunity did not come out of nowhere – for four quarters the lads from Lincoln had pressured, harassed and forced the Badgers into a corner from which there was only a narrow route for escape. Of course, it would have been no simple task for any team to score a touchdown in overtime away from home with a howling crowd firing up the other team. But the Huskers had succeeded against those odds for the previous 60 minutes, and they had earned their chance to win the game. It may have been nerves and a small amount of self-doubt that caused their final drive to come up short, but I hoped the players and coaches learned a couple of simple lessons from their trip to Camp Randall.

1. They are a good team that is capable of beating anyone outside the top four.
2. They deserve to beat teams like Ohio State and Iowa because their hard work has earned them that right.

Coming back to our earlier discussion about beating the odds in Las Vegas, in my view the Ohio State game offered one of the few sure bets that gamblers will ever find. Early in the week, the Buckeyes were 17+ point favorites to beat the Huskers. I guessed the bookmakers had been watching baseball last week instead of the Huskers game. Surely the brave Huskers would beat a 17-point spread. Heaven only knows what odds the bookies were offering against a Nebraska win – whatever they were, I thought it would not be a bad bet for any football fan.

A Nebraska win could easily cause the two teams to swap places on the ladder and turn the 6-9 upside down, so to speak.

Reasons to be Thankful

It looked like a beautiful night in Columbus on the evening of the game day Saturday. The stadium was packed with fans from both teams, and the memory of Sam Foltz was honored by Ohio State in a classy gesture that transcended college sports and reminded us all of our shared humanity. The stage was then set for a sporting event that would potentially have a great deal of impact on the fortunes of both the Buckeyes and the Huskers.

When my wife and I arrived at Vitty's Bar and Grill in Lewisville, TX a little later than we had planned, the only seats left untaken were a handful of chairs placed against the wall near two pool tables. The tables themselves had been covered with boards upon which a wide range of Nebraska souvenirs and clothing had been arrayed, including a number of t-shirts that had been designed by one of the co-owners of the bar, Blair native Bobby Vittitoe. Meanwhile his wife Gayle, dressed in her trademark cowboy hat and boots, greeted patrons at the door and handed them a ticket for the halftime raffle if they were able to show evidence that they were legally eligible to indulge themselves with the hallowed Nebraska tradition of a red beer.

Not long after we sat down, two clean-cut young men who looked like they had not long finished college appeared next to us and very politely enquired as to whether the three vacant chairs to our left were available. We replied that those chairs were indeed free and the young men gladly sat down and soon started talking animatedly with one another about the game ahead. The atmosphere in the bar was electric with the excited buzz of a crowd of 70-80 mostly fortyish men and women eagerly anticipating what promised to be an exciting game between two of the leading teams in the country. There was a full house at the stadium, a full house at the bar and the Nebraska fight song was playing on the jukebox.

In short, everything was in place for a very special evening.

And then a football game broke out and spoiled the night for the visiting team.

With the return of Carter to the lineup, the Three Huskerteers were back in action together for the first time in some weeks after recovering from their injuries. Right on cue, the first score of the night came on the third Huskers play from scrimmage.

After receiving the opening kickoff the Huskers ran a couple of plays, with Terrell Newby gaining a total of 7 yards, unfazed by the roaring home crowd of 108,750 (yes, you read that number correctly. Apparently up in Columbus they like to go watch their local football team). Armstrong dropped back to pass on the next play, only to see the ball tipped by a defender and knocked into the air. As the ball traced its graceful arc over the anxiously outstretched fingers of players from both teams, the crowd at Vitty's Bar held its collective breath, as I'm sure did all of the faithful Husker fans gathered at watch sites all across the country and in overseas locations such as Afghanistan and Australia. For a few moments, the frantic and frenetic flurry of the game seemed to become a slow-motion frame-by-frame imitation of its former self as thousands of pairs of eyes focused on the floating pigskin. Suddenly the ball landed in the hands of a Buckeye player and the world began to turn again. Freeze-frame had turned into super-speed, and before we knew what had happened the ball had been run back 36 yards and the Buckeyes had a 7-0 lead.

But looking on the bright side, the good news was that the Huskers would get the ball right back and could try again. And try they did, stringing together a 6-minute 16-play drive that stalled after 72 yards and ultimately resulted in a Drew Brown field goal. Even though the Buckeyes had stopped the Huskers on a first down from the two-yard line, the score was 3-7 and we had a game on our hands. Armstrong had completed 3 passes during the drive, while 6 other attempts fell incomplete due largely to excellent defensive plays by the Buckeyes. But the Huskers had shown that they could move the ball downfield, and the crowd of North Texas Nebraskans at Vitty's was excited for the game to resume after Brown's kickoff following the field goal.

If only the cable TV had gone out during the next commercial break we could have all gone home happy, because as the Sherpa Norgay Tensing was famously reputed to have said to the renowned mountain climber Edmund Hillary in 1953 a few seconds after they had become the first men ever to reach the summit of Mount Everest: "It's all downhill from here."

And so it was to be. The Huskers had reached their 2016 peak at number 6 in the rankings, only to lose narrowly to Wisconsin and fall 3 places. Personally, I felt this was simply a bump in the road for the Huskers and they would leapfrog over the Buckeyes by beating them in Columbus.

By the end of the first quarter, the Huskers trailed 3-14, but the Huskers had outgained the Buckeyes 103 yards to 90 and the mood remained upbeat among the fans crowded into the bar.

Around this time, an attractive college-aged young lady arrived and spotted the only vacant seat in the house which happened to be next to the two nearby young men who had been so focused on the game and talking to one another. The two gallant lads quickly made room for the new arrival to sit between them and, as far as I can tell, the two guys immediately became invisible to one another as each directed his attention entirely to the blonde newcomer for the remainder of the evening.

The crowd was still noisily encouraging the Big Red halfway through the second quarter despite another touchdown and field goal from the Buckeyes. But when the plucky quarterback Armstrong was knocked unconscious on the sideline after a rushing play, the noise level in the room suddenly changed from sounding like a loud ice hockey game to more like the muted hush of a golf tournament. Fortunately, he was not seriously injured, but with him leaving the game with the score 3-24 the prospects for his team did not look good. The rest, as they say, is history.

It seemed evident on the faces in the bar that all hope for a victory against the Buckeyes was carried off the field along with Tommy on his stretcher, and indeed a small portion of the crowd left during the halftime break while others were to drift away with glum faces during the third quarter.

Gayle bravely maintained her optimistic attitude throughout the remainder of the game, and by the time it was all over I wanted to join her in trying to look for the silver lining on the dark cloud that had descended on the bar and all of its patrons with the exception of a certain nearby pair of young men who seemed quite oblivious to the happenings on the screens all around them.

"Come on folks!" I would have said "Let's not allow something trivial like a 3-62 loss get us down! With the Thanksgiving holiday coming up, let's think about all the things we're grateful for. Okay, I'll start:

    1.   I'm thankful that I'm not a betting man.

2. I'm thankful that the Huskers' special teams got a lot of opportunities to practice their kickoff returns. (11 times to be exact).

3. I'm thankful it wasn't the worst Huskers loss ever. (It was only the second worst).

4. I'm thankful that I live too far away for a vengeful horde of flaming-torch-and-pitchfork-bearing Nebraskans to storm the Aussie Husker Fan's castle after I told them in my blog that the Huskers were a sure bet to beat the spread."

I'm also thankful that I didn't actually say any of the above out loud. Being on the receiving end of a knuckle sandwich would not have been a pleasant way to end my evening.

Your Guess is Better Than Mine

Overall it wasn't a good week for predictions from my point of view. First, the Buckeyes blew out the Las Vegas odds during their game against Nebraska, not only beating the eventual 15.5 point spread but also beating the over-under of 52 points with their own score. Then there was the little matter of the Presidential Election which took place that same week and saw Donald Trump confound the experts with his convincing win, contrary once again to my expectations. Given that most of the country was turned red by the Republican victory, I'm thinking that Husker fans ought to be able to petition the president-elect to strike the Ohio State game from the record books for the sake of uniting the nation and healing our collective wounds. Bob the Ticket Man seems to be pretty well-connected, so I quickly made plans to ask him before the next game if he could put me in touch with someone who knows someone. I'll keep you posted.

Although the Buckeyes game was difficult to watch in terms of the action on the field, the atmosphere at Vitty's bar remained exciting throughout most of the evening. Bobby and Gayle Vittitoe worked together as a team to create a lively and captivating ambiance, with Gayle using the PA system to encourage the crowd and Bobby adding to the mix via the jukebox. I am very happy to say that many of the 70-80 people in the crowd sang along with me when Bobby played the fight song before the game, and then the whole crowd sang along to "Sweet Caroline" and other songs of that same era during the halftime break while Gayle drew the raffle prizes.

Unfortunately, we never got the chance to sing the fight song again because the Huskers did not manage to score a touchdown, but judging from the joyful singing faces in the crowd one would never have known that their team was down 3-31 at the half and the quarterback was in the hospital. Full credit is due to the Vittitoes for creating a happy Nebraska family atmosphere in north Dallas that would be the envy of many of the watch sites that I have visited since the beginning of the 2001 season.

Looking back at the game, Ohio State was by far the better team and they deserved to win. It was similar in many ways to the previous game against Wisconsin, in which the Badgers looked like the better team. The difference was that while the Huskers were able to keep the Badgers off balance through a mixture of creative offense and solid defense, the Buckeyes stifled the Huskers offense while overrunning the defense. Although the Huskers were almost able to snatch a win in Madison, they were simply outclassed in Columbus as they recorded just 9 first downs in comparison to 34 by the home team. As much as I have lately become wary of making predictions, I don't think it's too much of a stretch to say that even if Armstrong had not been hurt, the Buckeyes would still have won by a large margin.

The good news for the Huskers was that Armstrong was not seriously hurt, and there were three more very winnable games remaining in the regular season in which the Huskers could bounce back.

That whole situation was much better than that faced by some other fierce competitors during the same week who would have to wait four more years before they could attempt to redeem themselves and make amends for their heartbreaking losses in the political arena.

CHAPTER TEN

TOM-MY OR NOT TOM-MY?

The question that weighed heavily on the minds of the widespread legions of Big Red Army for the 7 days leading up to the Minnesota game was whether their Field General Tommy Armstrong would gird himself up to face the slings and arrows of the Gophers after being concussed in the last game against the Buckeyes. Personally, I had no doubt that he should *not* play. In my view, it should be mandatory to sit out the next game following a concussion incident.

That was the rule that applied in my Australian Rules football days, and the standard treatment was to take the concussed player to the hospital where he would be kept overnight for observation. No exceptions allowed despite any and all objections by the patient. After leaving the hospital the player would not return to football practice for a few days, and body contact would be avoided until a week had passed. Full practice would resume the following week, and if all went well the player would be ruled available for the next game. In the case of the Huskers quarterback, the enforcement of this common-sense safety-first approach would mean that Tommy would not be available until the Maryland game the following week.

But common sense is not so common anymore, and that is exactly why I believed that Armstrong in his number 4 jersey would be taking the snaps against the Gophers.

After all, we're talking about a guy who not only signed himself out of the ER as soon as he possibly could, but who then came running back through the stadium to get to the sideline during the third quarter – still wearing his hospital scrub pants, for heaven's sake.

The Huskers were now 7-2 and the team badly needed him to help them get their season back on track by beating the Gophers in Lincoln after two hard losses on the road. As far as I could see, the only way that he would not be playing is if a band of hefty medical orderlies somehow found a way to strap him back on the same board that carried him into the ambulance last week. Even then there would likely be a popular uprising of Husker fans who would march on the ambulance, rescue their quarterback and carry him on their own shoulders to Memorial Stadium.

I knew my track record on predictions had been pretty miserable for the last week or so – the Buckeyes game and the Presidential election come to mind – but I was pretty sure that Armstrong would be third time lucky for me.

Speaking of luck, I had the good fortune during the previous few days to learn about a long-standing Husker tradition that was new to me. For the past three decades, Misty's Steakhouse and Lounge in Lincoln has hosted a pep rally on Friday nights during the football season and so I decided to take the opportunity to experience it for myself the night before the Minnesotas game. I had heard about this storied establishment from my wife, who had always wanted her parents to take her there during one of their visits to Lincoln while she was in college. However, despite her best lobbying efforts, they always took her somewhere closer to campus and less appealing to a college student. It therefore became my mission to scope out the scene at Misty's not only for my book but also for my dear wife who had been so sadly deprived of the Misty's experience through no fault of her own all those years ago.

I know what you readers are thinking, and I agree – it *was* indeed *very* noble of me to plan to spend an evening at the bar on my wife's behalf.

The parking lot on Havelock Avenue was full when I arrived at 6.15 on a cool evening, and once inside I found that the bar and lounge areas were even fuller. Not only were all the tables and chairs at the bar occupied, but there must have been 40 or more people standing around the large room waiting for a seat to open up. And there was plenty to entertain them as they waited because almost every corner seemed to contain some item of Husker memorabilia – not only related to football but

also other varsity sports including a large rowing shell suspended above the bar.

The atmosphere was jovial and good-natured while the wait staff contorted themselves around chairs, tables and customers of all ages as they carried trays laden with drinks and plates of Misty's signature prime rib

Fortunately for me, after about 15 minutes I was able to find a seat at the bar and sit back to absorb the lively scene. Soon afterward the two seats to my left became vacant and were quickly claimed by a pair of 30ish ladies who had been born and raised in Lincoln but now both lived in the Dallas area. Not only were they very familiar with Misty's, but one of them reported that this had been the venue for her wedding reception 15 years earlier. I didn't think to ask what color her bridesmaids wore, but I wouldn't be surprised if the after-dinner toast to the happy couple was made with red beer.

Shortly after 7pm a group of some 20 musicians and cheer-leaders descended into the room down a staircase, and added

their trombones, saxophones, clarinets, flutes, tuba and drums to the already noisy and crowded mix. After somehow snaking their way through the crowd they assembled to one side of the room where they proceeded to play a mixture of familiar songs and melodies for the next 20 minutes while Herbie the Husker looked on approvingly and greeted the many admirers who came to hug him and take selfies with this literally larger-than-life character.

Throughout it all, the cheerleaders maintained their smiles and even led a few cheers of their own. I was happy to see a few people singing along when the band played "Dear Old Nebraska U", although it seems that it was only the older generation who knew the words.

While this performance by the joyful ensemble was certainly entertaining, the intrepid musicians returned just after 8pm without cheerleaders and Herbie and then proceeded to line up standing on the bar right in front of me to play "Dear Old Nebraska U". I don't know whether anyone else in the

room was singing along, but I must say I have never been able to hear the melody so clearly!

Meanwhile, the lady on my left who had celebrated her wedding at Misty's recommended that I order the prime rib for dinner "Medium Rare" was best, she assured me. It wasn't long before I was presented with a large Texas-sized slab of meat on a plate that left scant room for items of lesser importance such as vegetables or salad.

Earlier in the day in Omaha, I had stopped for lunch at a Hy-Vee store near where my father-in-law had lived and where he and my wife and I had enjoyed several breakfasts together. When I asked the server behind the counter for his recommendation for something light for my midday meal he proceeded to serve me beef tips and gravy with mashed potatoes. Even though I had not been particularly hungry to begin with, the delicious tenderness of the meat awakened my slumbering appetite and I cleaned my plate from rim to rim.

On the way back to my hotel later that evening I reflected on the events of the day and realized that I had not seen a single vegetarian restaurant during any of my travels throughout the state. Vegans must be as rare in Nebraska, I thought, as Colorado fans and Democrats.

The next morning dawned bright and sunny, but by an hour before the 6.36pm kickoff, the mercury had dropped to 52 degrees. Worse news still for this fan visiting from a warmer clime was that the temperature was predicted to drop another 10 before the game was over. I wanted to blame the visiting Minnesota fans for bringing their weather with them but the first group I spoke to had driven up from Kansas City and flatly refused to take responsibility for the chilly conditions. My next Gopher interaction was with a group of 3 men who had driven down from Minneapolis. During the course of our conversation, they noted that this was their third visit to Lincoln, and I soon understood why they kept returning. On

their first visit, they had been struck by the friendliness of the Husker fans to the extent that they kept count of the number of times a Nebraska fan thanked them for coming. The final tally on that day was 26. Take a bow, Nebraska fans – you deserve it.

Just prior to the game, Coach Riley answered the question on everyone's lips when he announced during a radio interview that unless something untoward happened during the pre-game warm-ups, Armstrong would play. I'm not sure how far or wide that news had spread prior to the game, but anyone at the stadium who may still have been in doubt was treated on the giant video screens to the sight of number 4 in the locker room all suited up and ready to go as the Huskers prepared for their tunnel walk.

However, the anxious fans would have to wait a little while to see Tommy in action as the Golden Gophers had first use of the ball. And use it they did, marching 75 yards down the field in 14 plays to score a touchdown halfway through the first quarter. When it was finally Armstrong's turn to take the ball in hand he looked sharp as he took the team 36 yards down the field in 9 plays, culminating in a Drew Brown field goal. I'm sure I was not the only person in the 90,456-strong crowd who cringed when Armstrong's head was banged into the turf by a tackle during that opening drive, but he bounced back up and completed several passes and kept the ball moving. He later confessed at the post-game press conference that after the events of last week he had been a bit nervous about getting tackled heavily for the first time during this his next game, but when it happened he said he felt fine and his nervousness disappeared.

There were a good number of Minnesota fans in attendance and as the mercury fell I envied the two enterprising chaps who

wore furry head-to-toe golden gopher suits. Unfortunately, I was unable to get a picture of the toasty-warm pair, but they were far from the only fans in the crowd who displayed their team allegiance in unmistakable style.

The Huskers went on to score a touchdown before the end of the first quarter but remained behind 10-17 at the halftime break. It was during the third quarter that a collective groan resounded around the stadium after a pack of players cleared following a quarterback sneak play only to find Armstrong lying on the ground in distress. He had been at the bottom of a pile of bodies and I wondered if he had taken another blow to the head. Several trainers were quickly by his side and helped him off the field with an injured ankle as the crowd echoed the encouraging "Tommy! Tommy" chants of last week from the Ohio State crowd. Once again backup quarterback Ryker Fyfe stepped into the breach, but as we all know those Armstrong boots are hard to fill.

Armstrong remained off the field until 3 minutes into the final quarter with the score tied at 17. Despite a limp left over from his earlier ankle injury, here he was at his own 9-yard line ready to try to lead his team to victory. This would be a very challenging task for any quarterback, especially one with his mobility limited by a gimpy ankle. But Tommy was up to the task and led the team 78 yards through 12 plays to reach the Gophers 13-yard line. On the next play, he kept the ball and unreeled one of his signature zig-zag runs as he outpaced and outfoxed the defenders to sprint into the end zone for what would be the game-winning touchdown. It was only after reaching the back of the end zone that he began to favor his left leg and the crowd realized he had strained his left hamstring during the course of his creative running excursion.

It was a remarkable effort from Armstrong, especially when one stops to consider that at this same time 7 days earlier he had been strapped to a board in an ambulance on the way to hospital after being knocked unconscious. Once again he was

carried off the field, but this time there was no board involved and it was two of his teammates who did the lifting.

The final score of 24-17 broke the Huskers' two-game losing streak and improved their overall record to 8-2. Not only was there much relief in the stands that the Huskers were back on track, but the post-game press conference was attended by almost twice as many people and cameras than I had seen since Head Coach Mike Riley took over the program. Riley was smiling and looking quite relieved as he did his best to field questions from the reporters and journalists who frequently talked over one another in their eagerness to get his take on the game.

Jordan Westerkamp also made an appearance at the press conference after leading the receiver corps with 6 catches for 50 yards. But befitting his status as leader of the Three Huskerteers, he had once again modified his facial profile as he sported the beginnings of a goatee to go along with his flourishing mustache. Come to think of it, by virtue of his creative mixture of sideburns, mustaches and beards of different shapes and sizes I couldn't recall ever having seen Westerkamp exhibit the same facial configuration twice during the past two seasons.

The press was also eager to hear Tommy Armstrong's views on the game, and he tried hard to answer the multiple questions thrown his way despite being tired after throwing two touchdowns and running for a third. He reported that he was feeling good and that he was "Trying to stay healthy and move on to next week." To much relief all around, he went on to say that there was no way he would miss the next game against Maryland.

The final word belongs to Mike Riley, who had this to say after the game: "You all know Tommy….he is very, very competitive and doesn't ever like to come out of the game, and he always thinks he's gonna make the next play, which I really admire about him."

Husker fans everywhere would surely agree that Tommy has earned every ounce of that admiration.

CHAPTER ELEVEN

SUSPENSE ON SENIOR SATURDAY

"Can I imagine him not playing? I don't *want* to." Those were the words from Head Coach Mike Riley in the middle of the week between the games against Minnesota and Maryland when he was asked to speculate on whether Quarterback Tommy Armstrong would be available to take on the Terrapins for the Huskers' final home game of the 2016 season.

For the second week in a row, Husker fans were in the dark about Armstrong's prospects to take the field. Looking back at the previous week, not only had he been cleared on the morning of the Minnesota game to play that evening, but he also had turned in what was arguably his best performance of the year. His two passing and one rushing touchdown for the game drew him level with Eric Crouch for the highest total touchdowns (90) in school history and also earned him the honor of Big Ten Player of the Week.

However, the effort of completing 19 passes for 217 yards and rushing 9 times for another 61 took its toll on Armstrong's

body. Thankfully there was no repeat of the concussion he had
suffered a week earlier, but in this case it was Tommy's lower

body that suffered the brunt of the punishment he received in
return for his determination to lead the Big Red to victory. First
an ankle and then a hamstring.

I had first witnessed Armstrong's resilience last year when
I saw him on several occasions at the post-game press
conference with an ice pack strapped to his hamstring or a
walking boot on his ankle, yet he almost always rebounded to
play the next game. At last Saturday's post-game press
conference he literally guaranteed he would be back to take on
Maryland in his final home game as a Husker, and based on his
track record we in the assembled press corps had no reason to
doubt him.

There would be much to play for in the coming game
because defeating the Terrapins would give the Huskers an
undefeated season at home for only the second time since 2001.

It would also give the Huskers their 50th 9-win season and of course it would greatly improve their bowl ranking. Probably even more significantly, a win on Senior Day would also put a fitting capstone on what has been an emotional season following the untimely loss of punter Sam Foltz during the summer.

Ryker Fyfe could of course step in at quarterback in case Tommy was not fit to play, and I was fervently hoping that the coaches find a way to give him some playing time on his Senior Day even if Tommy was able to start. Fyfe practiced all week with the first-team while Armstrong was restricted to light throwing on Wednesday and sat out practice entirely on Thursday.

It seemed that Tommy's hamstring injury was more serious than he first thought after last week's game. According to Riley, intensive rehab efforts continued all week and the final decision about Armstrong's availability could come as late as Saturday morning.

Given that the game was scheduled for an 11am start, I hoped the team trainers and other decision-makers would be ready for an early start to their day. 28 Senior players and millions of Husker fans would be counting on them!

Meanwhile, there was nothing I could do except wait on the news from Huskers HQ, and since this was to be my final weekend in Nebraska for the season I felt I owed an allegiance to the man who had first sparked my interest in all things Nebraskan. I thus asked myself what my father-in-law would have done if he found himself with time on his hands on a Friday evening in Lincoln. The answer came to me almost instantaneously – he would go out and enjoy a steak dinner.

And so it was that I soon found myself at the Red Fox Steak House and Lounge, dining on a delicious bone-in ribeye and enjoying the sights and sounds around me as a mixture of what appeared to be regular customers and game-weekend visitors enjoyed a relaxed evening with friends while doing their best to avoid any possible risk of dying of thirst.

Just as I have usually found on occasions such as this when I have visited Nebraska, it wasn't long before I was able to engage in conversation with my neighbor in the seat next to me at the bar. However in this case, the middle-aged man seated next to me seemed to be somewhat distracted by two newspaper clippings placed in front of him on the bar. When I looked closer in the dim light I could see that he had cut out the crossword puzzle from two different newspapers, and he was trying to work on them in between drinking his beer, eating his dinner and keeping an eye on the college football game on the television behind the bar. As if he didn't have enough on his plate, so to speak, he kept up a regular dialog with the two attractive young female bartenders whom he tried to get interested in his word-finding hobby.

I must admit I had to give him credit for his creativity if he was trying to use the crossword puzzles as a means to meet a potential romantic partner. The closest I had ever come to such a ploy was in my elementary school days when one of the more worldly 11-year-old boys in my class would ask a girl on whom he had a crush if she could think of a four-letter word with one vowel that began with F and ended with K. (The answer, of course, is "fork". Oh, dear readers, what were *you* thinking?)

The multitasking crossword man seemed settled in for the evening and I left before he did, so I never got to see what would happen if he tried to impress one of the waitresses by calling her a positively poetic picture of pulchritude.

With game day just around the corner, I was anxious to see whether Tommy Armstrong's words from the last press conference would ring true or whether he had written a verbal check that his body was unable to cash.

Fyfe Beats the Drum

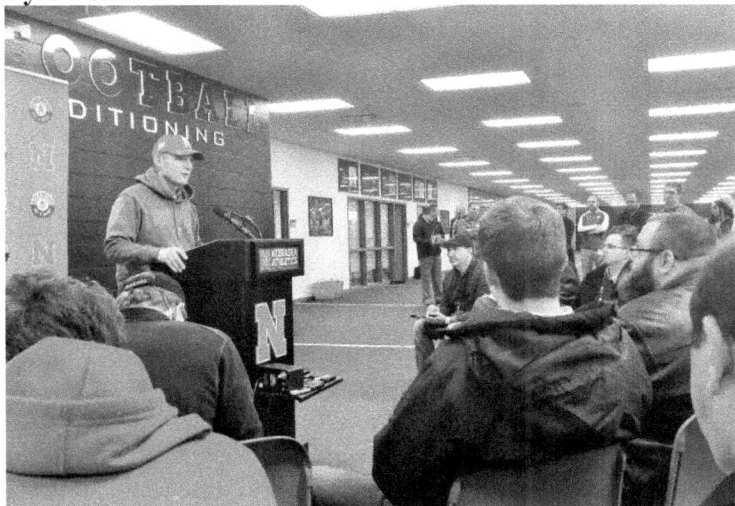

"I'm really proud of Ryker," said Head Coach Riley at the press conference after the senior from Grand Island started a game for the first time this season. Even without a formal survey or opinion poll of the fans, I can confidently say that there were 89,704 people in Lincoln who shared Riley's sentiment. Ryker Fyfe had been told by the coaches on the Sunday after the Minnesota game that he was very likely to be the starting quarterback against Maryland, and he should prepare himself accordingly. Somewhere in the back of his mind, he must have been thinking that he had heard all this before; that starting quarterback Tommy Armstrong was injured and might not be able to play the next week. In almost every case, the warning had turned out to be a false alarm as Armstrong was able to recover his fitness in time for the next game.

But in this case, it would potentially be something special for Fyfe in that he would be starting in front of his home crowd on Senior Day. Nevertheless, he must have been trying not to get too excited just in case the ever-resilient Armstrong was able to bounce back at the last minute to reclaim his starting place in the team. However, despite the best efforts of Armstrong and his trainers, the hamstring injury that was holding Tommy back did not recover sufficiently and thus Fyfe was told definitively on Thursday that the start would be his.

No doubt Fyfe was nervous to some degree about starting the game against Maryland, and I know many Husker fans were also extremely nervous given that the statistics from Fyfe's most recent extended outing against Ohio State were not very flattering in the midst of a 62-3 drubbing. But in all fairness, his 5 completions on 18 pass attempts for 52 yards were not that much different than Armstrong's numbers of 4 completions on 15 attempts for 74 yards, with both players recording one intercepted pass.

This was the backdrop to the game in which the Huskers would try to finish their series of home games unbeaten, and keep the door open for a 10-win regular season. The Three Huskerteers would all be present, although Ozigbo's ankle injury was still not quite healed. At the Senior ceremonies before the game, lead Huskerteer Jordan Westerkamp was visibly emotional and I'm sure many Husker fans were silently hoping that Armstrong would be dressed to play when he was introduced to the crowd.

But the stage was set and the onus would be on the Huskers' defense to do its part by restricting the scoring of the Terrapins offense, which had so far averaged some 215 rushing yards per game for the year. After the kickoff, the visitors had first possession of the ball and were held scoreless after failing to convert on 4th and 10. On the third play of Nebraska's first drive of the game, Fyfe completed a smooth 26-yard pass to Westerkamp as the crowd exhaled. Fyfe probably breathed a sigh of relief as well after that completion and another 10-yard pass later in this 9-play drive for 72 yards. He said after the game that Terrell Newby's touchdown on the 9th play of the drive had calmed his nerves and made him feel at ease. Scoring that early

touchdown certainly helped the crowd feel at ease, and I was inspired to celebrate by ordering my last Fairbury hot dog of the season.

Fyfe played very well and did not set a foot wrong in completing 23 out of 37 passes for 220 yards and a touchdown. Terrell Newby was outstanding, rushing for 98 yards and three touchdowns. However, the key to the game was the Huskers' defense that held the Terrapins' rushing attack to a net total of 11 yards on 25 carries. Not only that, but the defense recorded four sacks and held the Terrapins' time of possession down to 21 minutes for the game.

(I must confess I'm a little bit disappointed by that latter statistic because my experience with Nebraskans has always been that they are kind, generous and welcoming to visitors. But in this case, they invited that nice group of lads from the north-east to come down and play some football, and then did not share the ball fairly with them. Although on the other hand, it was a bit rude of those Marylanders to bring their 35-degree weather with them without fair warning.)

What we had witnessed in this game was a true team performance by the Huskers. I had been prepared to go on a rant about how lopsided football can be in general because it relies so heavily on the quarterback, but what I saw was that in the absence of their usual quarterback, the rest of this Big Red team stepped forward and shared the load together with their stand-in QB. Terrell Newby was a prime example of this team-centric mindset when he was asked after the game about his career-high three touchdown performance. Rather than taking credit for himself, he credited Fyfe and the offensive line for creating the conditions for him to succeed.

Although the 28-7 score was a little lopsided, it was a very enjoyable game to watch because it showed the depth of the Nebraska football program.

Once again I thought of my father-in-law Tom Hauser after the game as I enjoyed another steak dinner, this time at his favorite restaurant in Omaha. He would have been proud of his boys, and with a contented smile on his face he would have summed up the day in his succinct style: "That's Nebraska football. That's what they do."

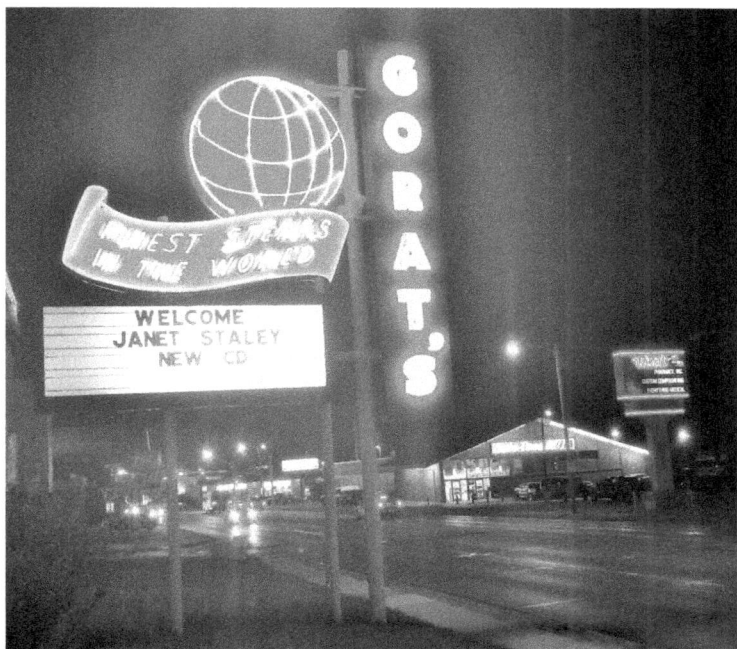

It was just a pity to think that 28 of the faces we saw in this game would be missing from the lineup next season. But there should be no regrets because they did themselves proud with Ryker Fyfe leading the way to a 9-2 record with one game remaining in the regular season.

CHAPTER TWELVE

THANKFUL THOUGHTS

Even an observer without the uncanny future-predicting skills of Johnny Carson's renowned seer Carnac the Magnificent would have had no problem predicting the outcome of the Huskers' final regular season game against the Iowa Hawkeyes in Iowa City. The home team's record was 7-4 going into the game, and they were unranked nationally. Meanwhile, Nebraska with its 9-2 record was ranked 19th in the nation after having been ranked as high as 7th prior to its two losses away from home against teams that were serious contenders for the 2016 National Championship playoffs.

The game was to take place the day after Thanksgiving, and the Huskers faithful were grateful for the fact that their quarterback Tommy Armstrong had recovered sufficiently from his injuries to take revenge on the Hawkeyes who had beaten Nebraska the year before and consigned them to a losing season. This was to be a new record for Nebraska, with Armstrong's 44th start eclipsing the 43 starts of his antecedent Taylor Martinez. Meanwhile, all three Huskerteers were fit and ready for the game and the Big Red were set to continue the trend of the past four seasons in which the visiting team had won the annual Nebraska-Iowa match-up each year.

Even though the Hawkeyes had beaten Michigan a few weeks earlier, it was not hard to envision the Great Carnac holding a sealed envelope to his elaborately turbaned and be-jeweled head and pronouncing in the most certain of tones the single word "Nebraska".

The anticipation leading up to the game reminded me of a saying used by the French: "One eats first with one's eyes". This principle explains much about the way food is served in French restaurants, where the servers will enlist extra help as needed to ensure that the dinner plates of all persons at a given table land in front of their intended recipient at the same time. On those rare occasions where there are insufficient servers to deliver all plates at the same time, the dishes arrive with covers on them and remain covered until all have been delivered and the covers can all be removed simultaneously by the team of servers with a dramatic flourish and a triumphant *"Voila!"* This creates an exotic effect similar to the pulling back of a curtain at a stage show to reveal a colorful and captivating set, eliciting a collective gasp from the audience. And as if this were not enough, the wait staff busily makes small adjustments to each plate on the table to rotate it and make sure the diner is pre-sented with the view of his or her intended meal in exactly the manner the chef intended.

Each diner is then expected to spend at least a few seconds gazing at the culinary vision in front of him and feasting his eyes before daring to reach for his silverware. To immediately pick up one's knife and fork without first appreciating the work of gastronomic art on the table is considered bad manners and an insult to the chef. And no matter whether the contents of the plate ultimately please each individual diner – especially those who may have misread the menu as I once did in France when I ordered *"les bulots"* in the belief that I was about to enjoy a Mediterranean delicacy of the rarest kind but instead was presented with a plate of boiled sea snails with a texture like rubber – he or she will at least have derived some pleasure from the anticipation prior to the event.

And so it was with the delicious anticipation leading up to the Hawkeyes game.

I would never compare the Huskers' on-field performance against Iowa to the disappointment I suffered from the plate of pencil erasers masquerading as the Special of the Day in that little seaside café, but the closest score of the day was at the kickoff and the Huskers went on to lose 10-40 after being held scoreless for the first and last quarters. It seemed that Armstrong was still suffering from the effects of his hamstring injury, and he finished the day with 13 pass completions from 35 attempts for 125 yards and a touchdown, and 13 rushing yards from 6 attempts.

Meanwhile, Chief Huskerteer Jordan Westerkamp's 4 receptions for 50 yards put him into second place on the Huskers' all-time receiving list with 167 receptions behind Kenny Bell with 181.

As unpalatable as the loss may have been to Husker fans on the day after Thanksgiving, the team's regular season record of 9-3 was still a far cry ahead of its unenviable 5-7 record after the 2015 Iowa game.

Continuing on with the theme of Thanksgiving and looking for the silver lining in every dark cloud, the Aussie Husker Fan was inspired to count his blessings and make a list of the things he's grateful for. In no particular order:

- I'm thankful for the strong academic performance of student-athletes that allowed the Huskers to go to the 2015 Fosters Farm Bowl.

- I'm thankful that the 2015 season is behind us.

- I'm thankful for Mike Riley, Tommy Armstrong and the players who bravely face the media at the post-game press conference each week, win or lose.

- I'm thankful for Tommy's ability to run the ball (when he is fit) as well as throw it.

- I'm thankful for Ryker's patience.

- I'm thankful for the Three Huskerteers: Westerkamp, Carter and Ozigbo.

- I'm thankful for Mike and Jen, and Jim and Shari for their generous tailgate hospitality.

- I'm thankful that my early-season suspicion about Jen being pregnant was correct.

- I'm thankful for red beer and Reuben sandwiches.

- I'm thankful for Bob the Ticket Man who always has a warm handshake for me and a pearl of wisdom to go along with a randomly-located seat somewhere in the stadium.

- I'm thankful for the man - who always seems to be seated behind me regardless of where I am in the stadium – who constantly offers advice out loud to the players, coaches and referees before and after each play.

- I'm thankful for the fans in front of me who sit for most of the game instead of standing.

- I'm thankful for the rented seat backs at Memorial Stadium. The best $5 I could ever spend.

- I'm thankful that I can watch Li'l Red stand on his head as the Huskers run out before the game.

- I'm thankful that I got to watch a game from the student section earlier this season.

- I'm thankful that my hearing is almost back to normal.

- I'm thankful for the thousands of red balloons that appear out of nowhere when the Huskers score their first touchdown of the game.

- I'm thankful for Fairbury hot dogs, Runza sandwiches and the 9-year-old children who sell them as they trudge up and down the concrete steps in the stands.

- I'm thankful that Nebraska's child labor laws apparently don't apply inside Memorial Stadium.

- I'm thankful for the University of Nebraska Marching Band.

- I'm thankful that no baton twirlers were trampled by a herd of stampeding tubas during the halftime break this season.

- I'm thankful for the hot water in the hand basins in the men's restrooms on a cold day.

- I'm thankful for the creative minds who design the countless different red t-shirts I see each week. Talk Herbie to me.

- I'm thankful for the Weiner Schlinger.

- I'm thankful that no-one has tried to deliver Valentino's into the upper stands by slingshot.

- I'm thankful for Gorat's, Cascio's, Red Fox, Misty's and their tasty Nebraska steaks.

- I'm thankful for the Sleep Inn in Omaha being located so close to the airport for my early Sunday morning flight home.

- I'm thankful for the unfailingly warm welcome I received from the residents of Aurora, Beatrice, Columbus, Fremont, Grand Island, Hooper, Kearney, Lincoln, Nebraska City, Norfolk, Omaha, Osceola, Scribner and Scottsbluff when I met them during my visits the day before a Huskers home game.

- I'm thankful for the two different Uber drivers in Lincoln who mailed back the reading glasses and iPhone that I left in their respective vehicles.

- I'm thankful for the joyful friendliness of the Nebraska fan clubs at watch sites in Dallas, Fort Worth, Orange, Laguna Hills, Lewisville, Oklahoma City, San Clemente and San Francisco.

- I'm thankful for anyone who sings "Dear Old Nebraska U" with me. Especially those who know at least a few of the words.

- I'm thankful that I have had the opportunity to explore Nebraska, its people and the NU football program for the past two seasons.

CHAPTER THIRTEEN

THE MOUTHFUL BOWL

While many Nebraska fans had held out hope that their Huskers would make it to one of the more prestigious bowl games, the loss against the Buckeyes doomed their chances of a trip to Florida or California. However, a 9-3 season was much to be thankful for and the pre-bowl speculation of 2016 was much less fraught than that of the prior season when the Huskers were fortunate to be able to play in the post-season at all with their 5-7 losing record.

Although Husker fans might have felt short-changed with the December weather in Nashville compared with Los Angeles or Miami, they more than got their money's worth with the convoluted title of their game: the "2016 Franklin American Mortgage Music City Bowl". The 9-3 Huskers would go into the game ranked 24th in the nation and would take on the unranked Tenessee Volunteers with their 8-4 record.

The Vols' season had been somewhat similar to that of the Huskers', in that they had climbed as high a number 9 in the national rankings before suffering some losses against highly-ranked teams and tumbling to 24th place for their final game.

And just like the Huskers, the Vols had lost their last game of the regular season against one of their regional rivals.

Both teams were clearly anxious to end their season on a winning note, but the Vols were listed as favorites since the Huskers would be without the services of Tommy Armstrong who had still not recovered fully from the torn hamstring injury he had suffered some 7 weeks earlier in the game against Minnesota.

Ryker Fyfe would thus start at quarterback for the Huskers, but the team would be without the services of lead Huskerteer and facial hair living canvas Jordan Westerkamp who injured his knee at practice a couple of weeks before the bowl game and underwent surgery that would sideline him for 3 months. It was unfortunate news for the wide receiver who was just 6 receiving yards away from moving into second place on the Nebraska career receptions list. Despite missing two games earlier in the season due to a back injury, he still led the team with 38 receptions, 526 receiving yards and 5 touchdown receptions.

The game was scheduled for a 12.30 start Pacific time on Friday, December 30th, which altogether created the conditions for a perfect workday in my mind. I would just go to the office in the morning as usual, and then call it a day (and a year) at noon which would allow just enough time to drive the few miles to Danny K's Billiards and Sports Bar and get set up among the Huskers faithful with a red beer in my hand before the kickoff.

When I arrived I found about 40 members of the Californians for Nebraska gathered for the game. Another 20 or so trickled in during the first quarter - no doubt after having experienced the same stress-free workday as me. I made a mental note to suggest to my boss that my department should adopt this new schedule after the New Year, but then I thought better of the idea. We should instead implement this new routine for the entire month of December with all of its Bowl games. Considering all of the time, effort and expense put forth by the schools and sponsors to create this rich and exotic smorgasbord of games at the end of the season, it only seems fair that we should watch as many of those matchups as possible unconstrained by the petty distractions of work.

Contented in my mind with this brilliant and can't miss plan, I turned my attention back to the game.

The first quarter was pretty much a stalemate, with the two teams trading field position but unable to score. Fyfe had completed 2 of his 5 pass attempts for a total of 10 yards, while the Huskers struggled a little with their ground game, gaining only 24 yards on 11 carries. On the other side of the field, the Vols had gained 23 yards on 5 of 10 pass attempts, but rather more ominously had gained 51 yards on only 4 rushes.

The crowd was in a good mood at the quarter-time break when I had the opportunity to reconnect with Michael and Monica whom I had met earlier in the season - a couple of fans like myself who were not born in Nebraska but joined the Big Red Army as soon as they could.

Michael was born in California and attended UNL in the mid-90s, which is where he had formed his allegiance to the Huskers, while Monica was a Louisiana girl who was converted to the Cornhusker cause through her marriage to Michael. But when she told me about her Christmas tree I was quickly reminded of the old saying that you can take the girl out of Louisiana but you can't take Louisiana out of the girl. In a creative home decorating move that would have made Martha

Stewart proud, just 5 days after Christmas Monica had already converted her tree from one season to the next – it was now a Mardi Gras tree. I had never heard of such a thing, but who am I to doubt the word of someone raised in the home of the Hurricane and Café Brûlot? *Laissez les bons temps rouler.*

And the good times were indeed rolling for Michael in 1994 while he was home in Los Angeles from college and watched on TV as the Huskers won the national championship in Miami. As much as he enjoyed seeing the game and watching his team win the title, he felt a certain emptiness that he was not in Lincoln to celebrate the victory with his friends and classmates. He vowed then and there not to make the same mistake the following year if the Huskers were in the running for the national title.

As things turned out, the Huskers were indeed in the running in 1995 and so Michael made sure to stay in Lincoln to watch the game from Arizona with friends. After the game was over and the Big Red had won a resounding 62-24 victory, someone in the room said: "Let's go downtown!" And so they did.

Michael recalls that the traffic in Lincoln was at a standstill, but that was just perfect for him as he was then able to run up and down P Street giving high fives to car drivers and their passengers. Then someone said: "Let's go to the stadium!" And so they did.

The gates at the stadium had been opened and by the time they arrived the field was crowded with ecstatic Nebraska fans celebrating their team's back-to-back national titles. Then someone said: "Let's pull down the goalpost!" And so they did.

As the crowd on the field continued to grow, Michael decided to make his way out of the stadium. But caught in the

www.ingramcontent.com/pod-product-compliance
Lightning Source LLC
Chambersburg PA
CBHW052007090426
42741CB00008B/1584